D0866469

PEACEFUL CHANGE

PUBLICATIONS OF THE

COUNCIL ON FOREIGN RELATIONS

FOREIGN AFFAIRS, a quarterly review, edited by Hamilton Fish Armstrong.

SURVEY OF AMERICAN FOREIGN RELATIONS, prepared under the direction of Charles P. Howland. Volumes for 1928, 1929, 1930, and 1931.

THE UNITED STATES IN WORLD AFFAIRS (*annual*). Volumes for 1931, 1932 and 1933 by Walter Lippmann and William O. Scroggs. Volumes for 1934-1935 and 1936 by Whitney H. Shepardson and William O. Scroggs.

POLITICAL HANDBOOK OF THE WORLD (*annual*), edited by Walter H. Mallory.

THE FAR EASTERN CRISIS, Recollections and Observations, by Henry L. Stimson.

RAW MATERIALS IN PEACE AND WAR, by Eugene Staley.

WHY WE WENT TO WAR, by Newton D. Baker.

CAN WE BE NEUTRAL?, by Allen W. Dulles and Hamilton Fish Armstrong.

INTERNATIONAL SECURITY, by Philip C. Jessup.

ORES AND INDUSTRY IN SOUTH AMERICA, by H. Foster Bain and Thomas Thornton Read.

ORES AND INDUSTRY IN THE FAR EAST, by H. Foster Bain.

THE RECOVERY OF GERMANY, by James W. Angell.

EUROPE: THE WORLD'S BANKER, 1870-1914, by Herbert Feis.

THE FOREIGN POLICY OF THE POWERS, by Jules Cambon, Richard von Kühlmann, Sir Austen Chamberlain, Dino Grandi, Viscount Ishii, Karl Radek, and John W. Davis.

FOREIGN AFFAIRS BIBLIOGRAPHY, 1919-1932, by William L. Langer and Hamilton Fish Armstrong.

DIRECTORY OF AMERICAN AGENCIES CONCERNED WITH THE STUDY OF INTERNATIONAL AFFAIRS, compiled by Ruth Savord.

PEACEFUL CHANGE

A Study of International Procedures

BY

FREDERICK SHERWOOD DUNN

YALE INSTITUTE OF INTERNATIONAL STUDIES

COUNCIL ON FOREIGN RELATIONS

45 EAST 65TH STREET, NEW YORK

Printed in the United States of America

FOREWORD

The Tenth International Studies Conference, scheduled to meet in Paris on June 28, 1937, has chosen as its subject for discussion "the Peaceful Solution of International Problems—Peaceful Change." The institutions represented in the Conference are submitting reports on various aspects of this topic, with their investigation centered on matters of population, colonies, markets and raw materials. The study submitted herewith is concerned with all such questions, but it deals with them with a somewhat different objective from that followed in most of the other reports.

The purpose here is not so much to present factual material as to relate the material in other reports, especially in those submitted to the Conference by the American group, to methods of procedure for relieving international tension created or presumed to be created by population pressure, lack of access to raw materials, restrictions on trade, and so forth.

Historical background and political and economic diagnosis are essential to an understanding of the problems involved in peaceful change, but after the information is at hand there still remains the question of putting it to practical use. The statistical exhibits should not only be accurate; they should be helpful in constructing a workable peace system.

The American studies have been prepared under the general supervision of an American Coördinating Committee for International Studies, which assigned the task of planning the documentation for the Conference to a special Committee of Experts under the chairmanship of James T. Shotwell. The cost of research and publication has been met by a generous grant from the Rockefeller Foundation. The preparation of a study of procedural methods of peaceful change was placed under the direction of a subcommittee composed as follows: John Foster Dulles (chairman), Frederick S.

Dunn (rapporteur), Hamilton Fish Armstrong, Philip C. Jessup, and Walter Lippmann.

While the members of this subcommittee have sought to be helpful with suggestions, they have not attempted to influence the opinions of the author of this study. He alone is responsible for the presentation of facts, arguments and conclusions. Although members of the subcommittee do not necessarily endorse every statement appearing herein, they accept the document as a whole for presentation to the International Studies Conference as an analysis from an American point of view of the procedures of peaceful change.

The author gratefully acknowledges the assistance of the members of this subcommittee and of members of the subcommittees on population problems and raw materials. His thanks are due to the Yale Institute of International Studies for releasing him temporarily from other work while preparing this study. His colleagues, Professor Nicholas J. Spykman and Professor Arnold Wolfers, have made many helpful suggestions. He is particularly indebted to Miss Helen M. Moats of the research staff of the Yale Institute for her untiring assistance in the preparation of the study. The research staff of the Council on Foreign Relations has likewise been most helpful.

FREDERICK S. DUNN

May 10, 1937.

CONTENTS

CHAPTER ONE

PEACEFUL CHANGE AND NATIONAL POLICIES

THE things for which nations profess to fight are of two kinds: those which they believe they are entitled to as a matter of law, and those which they do not claim as of legal right but want on some other ground. When a nation becomes involved in a dispute with another nation, it is either seeking to have its share in the existing distribution of rights and possessions confirmed and protected, that is, to maintain the status quo, or it is seeking to have the status quo changed.

In the attempt to construct a workable peace system after the World War, special attention was devoted to the settlement of disputes of the first type. To this end, steps were taken toward strengthening the habit of law observance among nations, establishing adequate judicial machinery for deciding claims of legal right, improving and extending the scope of international law, and guaranteeing the preservation of the status quo by the collective action of the international community. The general assumption underlying these moves was that the problem of war and peace was essentially one of protecting legal rights against potential lawbreakers.

The events of recent years have shown this assumption to be only partly true. The most dangerous threats to peace have in fact arisen out of disputes of the second type, that is, out of claims to change the status quo, not to uphold it. Thus in the Japanese action in Manchuria, the Italian conquest of Ethiopia and the remilitarization of the Rhineland by Germany, the country initiating the action in each case was not seeking to obtain its legal rights but was seeking to alter the existing legal situation. In the absence of effective international procedures for meeting their desires, the nations concerned resorted to force or the *fait accompli.* The results were brilliantly successful from their standpoint but disastrous for the peace system as a whole. The break-down of that system has made it clear that no peace system can be expected to work for any length of time unless it contains adequate provision for bringing about changes in the status quo as required by changing conditions.

The term "peaceful change," then, refers simply to the alteration of the status quo by peaceful international procedures rather than by force. The "status quo" is the existing distribution of rights and possessions as established or recognized by the legal system. In the international field, this means primarily territorial distribution, since, through the operation of the concept of sovereignty, dominion over territory carries with it practically all other things which nations desire to possess. But the status quo also includes any situation established by treaty or by international law, whether a part of the territorial distribution or not. Thus it would include limitations on the internal freedom of action of a state established by a treaty, for example, the demilitarization of the Rhineland. Any peaceful procedure for altering either the existing territorial distribution or the status of any nation would be regarded as a procedure of peaceful change. In brief, peaceful change is concerned both with changes in the distribution of rights and possessions and changes in the laws which govern the acquisition of rights and possessions.

Current discussion of peaceful change is centered primarily on the demand of Germany for the return of her colonies. Less pressing at the moment because already gratified in large part are the claims of Japan and Italy for more territory in order to relieve their population pressures. Italy admits that she is a "satiated" state for the time being, while digesting her new African Empire, but Japan is already stressing her need for greater access to raw materials and markets. Of the other Powers, Poland seems to be preparing to come forth with demands for changes in the status quo as a means of relieving her population pressure, and Hungary is permanently dissatisfied with the territorial settlements of the peace treaties.

The popular current grounds, then, for demanding changes in the status quo are three: (1) the need for greater access to supplies of raw materials and to markets for the disposal of surplus manufacturers; (2) relief from population pressure; and (3) the restoration of territories lost through conquest. Of these, the first two have received the widest response from the public and have been pressed the hardest by the Powers dissatisfied with the status quo. These two grounds have formed the basis for a general theory of international politics which at the moment is enjoying great popularity, especially in the dissatisfied countries. This is the theory of the "Haves" and the "Have-nots."

The Haves and the Have-nots

As its name implies, the theory is based on the patently uneven distribution of people and natural resources among the nations of the world. Everyone is aware, for example, that a very large portion of the human race is concentrated in a comparatively small number of states on the European continent while vast territories in other parts of the world are not supporting nearly as many people as they could easily be made to support. In the matter of raw materials the unevenness of the distribution is even plainer. A few Powers have more than they need of nearly everything, while the remaining states of the world are dependent on outside sources for many of the things essential to the existence of their peoples.

The "Haves," according to this theory, are the United States, the British Empire, Soviet Russia and France. These countries have succeeded, largely by conquest, in achieving a sufficiency in land and raw materials for their populations, both present and prospective, and their policy is accordingly aimed at maintaining the status quo at all costs. The "Have-nots," which, until recently at least, included Germany, Japan and Italy, are suffering from overpopulation and a serious shortage of raw materials and cannot have any sense of security until these needs have been met, preferably through the acquisition of additional territory. Hence, according to the theory, there is bound to be conflict, the Have-nots struggling to get the minimum conditions of existence and the Haves struggling to hold on to what they have. The existing peace machinery, especially the League of Nations, cannot be expected to cope with this situation because it is controlled by the Haves, which are the stronger group at the moment, and is used primarily to fortify the existing division of territory. The essential instability of the present situation apparently can only be cured by the Haves yielding to the territorial demands of the Have-nots.

This theory is very plausible on the surface and

can readily be supported by charts and figures on raw materials and population. However, there are several things wrong with it. In the first place, some of the nations listed as Have-nots turn out on investigation to be very much better off in the matter of population pressure and raw materials than many nations which do not seek additional territory. It is true, for example, that Germany has only one-fifth as much arable land per inhabitant as has the United States, but she is very much better off in this respect than Switzerland or Czechoslovakia or many other nations which do not complain of overpopulation. It is also true that Italy has no coal, but neither have most of the republics of South America. There is in fact considerable suffering from population pressure in various areas in the United States, a leading power among the Haves, in spite of its very low ratio of population to arable land. It has not in fact been established that the so-called Have-not nations cannot support their populations on the land which they now have, or that they cannot obtain in the open market all the raw materials they need for peace-time purposes.

But the chief difficulty with the theory is that it starts from the assumption that national economies must be self-sufficient systems, *i. e.,* that each nation should be able to get from its own territory the food and raw materials necessary for the support of its inhabitants. In fact, so far as peace-time conditions are concerned, there is little foundation for this assumption. If it were possible to keep the channels of trade open, the actual location of sources of raw materials would be a matter of relative indifference. The effort at national self-sufficiency means losing the advantages of specialization and is almost certain to result in a lower standard of living. Any theory which looks upon nations as closed economic units appears to ignore the manner in which the present industrial civilization has developed. With the devices that have been invented for trading across national boundaries, there is no necessary reason why trading areas should correspond with the limits of political jurisdiction, and there are many reasons for not trying to make them do so. On the other hand, the break-down in the system of international trade in recent years undeniably gives the Have-nots a talking point for self-sufficiency. However, unless it is assumed that this break-down is permanent, the case for self-sufficiency does not hold.

In brief, while the theory of the Haves and Have-nots undeniably contains a degree of truth, it is also to a large extent misleading. On the one hand, it is perfectly true that there is a wide diversity in the relative positions of the Powers considered as economic units, and that those which have control over sources of raw materials have advantages over those without such sources. It is likewise true that the nations advantageously situated in this respect are very anxious to maintain the status quo and that those less well situated are equally anxious to bring about a redistribution. On the other hand, it does not appear that the peace-time economic life of the so-called Have-nots has as yet actually been crippled by their lack of control over sources of raw materials, nor is it at all clear that, even if such were the case, a redistribution of territory would be the appropriate remedy.

In fact, the reasons which impel nations to seek changes in the status quo are far more complex than the above theory suggests. Governments are of course concerned with improving the peace-time economic condition of their peoples, but it is impossible to explain solely on that ground the various territorial changes that have been sought in the past. There are other ends which nations seek through changes in the status quo, ends which are seldom publicly announced but which are almost universally regarded as more important than that of a high standard of living for their people in peace time. Unless these ends are taken into account it is not possible to deal intelligently with the question of peaceful change.

Power Politics

The first of these ends is power. The most pervasive fact about the relations of nations today is the prevalence of what is generally known as power politics. There is a constant and vigorous struggle among them to achieve some relative power advantage over others. The most obvious outward manifestation of this struggle is the incessant competition in armament. But power politics is equally present in the struggle for territories, for raw materials and markets and various other objectives of foreign policy. In the case of some nations, it takes precedence over all other aspects of foreign relations, including the economic and social welfare of the population in peace time.

The term "power politics" has a sinister sound, and there is a widespread tendency to regard governments which practice it as bad governments and to explain their preoccupation with it as due to "militarism" or some other moral defect. Actually it seems an inevitable accompaniment of the kind of organization that exists in the international community today. That organization is still based in large measure upon the notion of "self-help," which means that the individual members of the community must eventually rely upon their own strength to defend their rights and possessions or to obtain what they want. So long as this expectation exists, government officials may be counted on to try to place their own nation in as strong a position as possible in reference to other nations against which they might have to use their strength. If they did not do so they would probably not remain in office very long.

Power in this sense means the ability of a nation to make its will prevail over other nations which have conflicting interests. It is characteristic of each nation to believe that its own possession of power is for just and enlightened purposes only, whereas the possession of power by others is very likely for purposes of aggression. Of course if a state were able to rely with confidence on the institutions of the international community to protect it in its rights and possessions or to fulfill its needs, it might refrain from building up its own strength. But the extent of power competition among nations today is an accurate measure of the lack of confidence which they have in the ability of international institutions to afford them such protection.

Hence power, which is in fact only a means to enable a state to attain its objectives, becomes itself a major objective of policy. Nations claim things as necessary to their vital interests which in fact are necessary only to build up their power to impose their will upon others. Thus it comes about that the things which nations value most highly, and for which they are most readily apt to go to war, are the things which bear upon their power to make war.[1]

[1]"When I say that the principal cause of war is war itself, I mean that the aim for which war is judged worth while is most often something which itself affects military power." R. G. Hawtrey, *Economic Aspects of Sovereignty* (London, 1930), p. 107. On the general subject of the rôle of power in international affairs, see Frederick L. Schuman, *International Politics* (New York, 1933), pp. 505-532.

The result of this is a great confusion of values and of attitudes. Things which are valued highly in terms of the national good have often very little to do with the existence and welfare of the people in time of peace. In fact they may be quite detrimental to that welfare. Thus nations have in the past gone to war to obtain territory needed to give them strategic frontiers, but in acquiring such territory they have at the same time set up irredentist problems which have been a constant source of irritation in peace time and have forced them into extensive military preparation in order to defend their acquisitions. Or again, a nation may lack a particular raw material that is useful both in peace and in war, such as petroleum. This material may be readily available in time of peace but there may be doubts about obtaining a continuous supply in war time. The acquisition of foreign territory containing the material is apt to be an objective highly valued by the people of this country, although they contemplate no war and although the acquisition of the territory might constitute a very heavy burden in peace time. Frequently those who determine government policy are not at all clear in their own minds as to why they seek a particular alteration in the status quo, whether it is necessary for the peacetime welfare of the people or whether it is for the purpose of building up the war-time strength of the nation.

This confusion of values is of great significance for the problem of peaceful change. For power is relative. The strength of one nation can only be measured in terms of the relative weakness of competing nations. Each nation constantly seeks to achieve such an appearance of power that the demands of its representatives will be listened to with respect by other nations. Preparedness for war is meaningless except in terms of the relative degree of preparedness of those states against which one is preparing. Hence foreign policy becomes directed toward the acquisition of things which enhance state power, and the people attach emotional values to these things quite apart from their effect upon the peace-time standard of living of the country.

The bearing of all this on the problem of peaceful change is clear. All proposals for changes in the status quo, regardless of the grounds on which they are based, are bound to be assessed first and foremost in terms of their effect upon the power relationships of the nations concerned. Any proposed change which would noticeably alter the existing power ratio to the disadvantage of any state is fairly certain to be resisted tenaciously, regardless of the justice of the claim or of its bearing upon the general welfare of the community. This point cannot be emphasized too strongly. So long as the notion of self-help persists, no nation will willingly agree to a change which will impair its ability to defend its position in a clash with other states. Hence it is idle to try to devise procedures for bringing about such changes peacefully, unless these procedures frankly embody the notion of coercion by marshaling an overwhelming force behind the proposed change.

Of course nations practically never seek changes in the status quo openly for the purpose of increasing their war potential at the expense of other states. Such claims are always advanced on some more palatable grounds. But whatever the real objectives may be, the possible effect of the change on power relationships will be closely scrutinized, and if the effect is perceptible it will be stoutly resisted. This is merely to say that so long as the notion of self-help persists, the aim of maintaining the power position of the nation is paramount to all other considerations. Questions of abstract justice or of internal needs, or demands for equality and independence cannot be expected to prevail over considerations of national power and security.

This situation inevitably limits the possibilities open to procedures of peaceful change. Where power considerations enter in, it becomes difficult if not impossible to consider claims for changes on their merits. If a claim has palpable merit aside from the power question, then it is apt to receive due consideration only under four conditions: (1) if it is presented by a strong Power against a weak

Power; (2) if it is presented by a weak Power actively supported by one or more strong Powers; (3) if it is presented against a Great Power by an alignment of Powers representing an overwhelming force; (4) if guarantees can be worked out which in effect nullify the power consideration. Otherwise the only possibility is to find some other means of satisfying the needs of the claimant state than by granting the change demanded.

It is of course possible to exaggerate the importance of power considerations in determining the course of international events. There are large areas of international relations in which power considerations play no particular part. In many fields common interests have grown up and common institutions have in large part supplanted the previous competitive struggle for national advantage. It may be anticipated that international institutions for the protection and adjustment of rights and possessions will steadily become more effective and that nations will gradually place more confidence in these institutions and less in their own strength, thereby reducing the importance of power politics. But in the meantime it must be expected that all proposals for alterations in the status quo will first be scrutinized from this standpoint, and those which are designed to give a nation a power advantage over others, or which, although conceived in terms of peace-time needs, would nevertheless upset the existing power relationships, will be strongly resisted.

Prestige

Another common ground for seeking changes in the status quo is the desire to enhance the prestige of a nation. This desire is at once one of the most pervasive of aims and one of the least understood. To take pride in the glory of one's country and to seek to enhance that glory is commonly accepted as one of the most commendable of virtues. Yet when this attitude finds expression in plans for national expansion at the expense of other nations or in a unilateral voiding of treaty obligations regarded as detrimental to national pride or ambition, it becomes one of the most serious threats to the general peace and welfare of the international community.

Prestige as a goal of national policy is often spoken of as if it were an end in itself. But in fact it is usually a means to some other more specific end. Prestige most generally means *reputation for power.*[2] As such it is but a phase of the competition for power mentioned above. It is a means toward making the national will prevail in dealings with

[2]"War means the imposition of the will of the stronger on the weaker by force. But if their relative strength is already known, a trial of strength is unnecessary; the weaker will yield to the stronger without going through the torments of conflict to arrive at a conclusion foreknown from the beginning. The reputation for strength is what we call *prestige.*" Hawtrey, *op. cit.*, p. 95. Italics in original.

other nations. For this purpose prestige is sometimes more important than actual physical power itself. For it is not so much the real military strength of a nation which determines how much weight its diplomatic representations will carry in the foreign offices of other nations, but the conception which other nations have of its power and its willingness to use it. Nations dissatisfied with the status quo will tend to do everything possible to increase their prestige in the hope that their demands for change will be received by other nations with greater respect.

There have been many examples in recent years of the building up of prestige as a prelude to seeking a more influential voice in the councils of nations. It is no secret that Italian policy from the Corfu incident down to and including the conquest of Ethiopia has been directed primarily toward increasing Italy's reputation for power. *Il Duce* has on many occasions recalled the fact that Italian claims at the Peace Conference were ignored because Italian prestige had fallen to a low ebb. He accordingly set out to build up that reputation at any cost. So successful was he in this quest that Great Britain hesitated in 1935 to challenge the sincerity of his intentions to fight it out. He is reported to have said in the course of the Ethiopian adventure that even if Ethiopia were handed to him on a silver platter he would not take it since he was determined to seize it by force as a demonstration of the new Italian military strength. Whether he actually said this or not, it can scarcely be denied that he has succeeded brilliantly in enhancing Italy's reputation for power, and that, as a result, Italian claims are received with far more respect today than in 1920. A somewhat similar story could be told regarding the prestige of Germany since the Nazi régime came to power. The actual extent of German rearmament is a closely guarded secret, but it is undeniable that Germany's reputation for power has vastly increased in recent years. It is also clear that the armament program which the British Government has announced in such impressive terms to the rest of the world is for the purpose of restoring British prestige in international councils after the British set-back in the Ethiopian incident. The immense utility of prestige in influencing the course of international events has been demonstrated many times in recent years.

So long, then, as power considerations continue to play an important part in the relations of nations, so long will individual nations seek to enhance their prestige, *i.e.,* the opinion which others have of their fighting strength. But it is clear that any proposals for altering the status quo which have as their aim to increase the prestige of a particular state could hardly form a suitable subject for procedures of peaceful change. For to build up a nation's prestige is to build up its bargaining power, and any nation which would be placed at a disadvantage thereby could be counted on to resist the move. Furthermore, the chief way in which a nation builds up its reputation for fighting power is by its own individual action taken without the approval of the international community. Hence it would hardly seek to increase its prestige through voluntary international procedures.

Honor

But it is argued that this is only one aspect of the problem of prestige, and that there is also a different kind of prestige sought by nations which is not directly concerned with power relationships but is more like the personal honor of private individuals. It is perfectly true that nations are often greatly concerned over the amount of respect paid to them by other nations, and that they are quick to resent any intentional slight or insult or any failure to observe the appropriate ceremonials. It is likewise true that nations, like individuals, can feel humiliation over suffering defeat in war or diplomacy, and that if forced to accept a status which they do not regard as in accord with their size or cultural development, they will be resentful and dissatisfied until they are able to effect a change. Where defeat in war is accompanied by loss of territory, such territory is apt to become a symbol of national humiliation, and the preservation of national self-respect becomes dependent upon the possibility of recovering the territory.

It is often maintained that this is the type of prestige which Germany is concerned with at the present time, and not merely with her reputation for power. Thus it is said that one of the important reasons why she wants her colonies back is, not to increase her military and economic strength, but merely to put herself on a plane of equality with the other Great Powers, all of which have extensive dependencies. In support of this position it is argued that taking away her colonies was in the form of a punishment, that it was an indication that she was not worthy to have colonies, and her desire now is to escape from this humiliating position. This can be done either by getting back her lost colonies or by the other Powers giving up their colonies to some form of international control in which she participates on an equal basis.

It may be admitted that a nation can be concerned about her honor or prestige without being conscious of the relationship between it and power. It is not easy, however, for other nations to make the separation. In the first place, the ceremonials and symbols of respect which nations are concerned about are in the end merely signs of rank or relative status. Rank among nations is inevitably associated with relative power. Hence the signs of respect which nations demand are primarily acts of recognition by others of the particular place in the power scale to which a nation believes itself entitled. Accordingly, although the people of a nation may not be immediately conscious of the fact that their desire to have their nation respected is a desire to have her power position acknowledged, the connection is there just the same.

But whatever we may call the feeling, it is true that nations which have been defeated in a trial of strength and have lost influence thereby will desire very strongly to recover their former position. If they cannot recover their actual power position they will at least desire the outward marks of that position. Where the terms of settlement imposed on a defeated Power force upon it a position of inferiority that is noticeably out of line with its size and cultural development relative to other nations, it can be depended upon to seek to escape from that position by every possible means, and its signature to a treaty will not be a bar to such action.

It is widely believed that the terms of the Treaty of Versailles imposed such a position on Germany; at any rate a large part of the German population seems to feel so. Hence it could be confidently predicted that Germany would resort to any necessary means to recover her former position among the Great Powers. She has succeeded in recovering a large part of her lost position, chiefly through ignoring the internal limitations on her sovereignty and through the method of the *fait accompli.* But she still regards the loss of her colonies as a major symbol of the inferior position which the peace settlement sought to impose upon it. This would probably continue to be the case even if the problems of raw materials and markets could be taken care of in some other manner. One may accordingly predict continued effort on the part of Germany to recover her colonies quite apart from the question of the effect of such recovery on Germany's economic welfare or even on her military power.

Hence if peace is desired, it would seem important to try to devise some way in which this remaining symbol of German defeat can be removed without at the same time unduly upsetting the power balance which the victorious Powers regard as necessary to their security. But Germany also demands the return of her colonies on other grounds besides national honor. More particularly she wishes them in order to provide access to raw materials and markets as well as for expansion for her population. Hence it will be well to postpone consideration of the possibility of satisfying her demands until some attention has been given to these grounds for alterations in the status quo.

Self-Sufficiency

Before considering these special grounds for demanding changes it is necessary to take note of another general objective of national policy which is particularly strong in some countries and is often associated with claims for raw materials and markets. This is self-sufficiency. The notion of self-sufficiency is nearly as incompatible with the notion of international procedures of peaceful change as is the notion of national power. In fact the chief reason for seeking self-sufficiency is national power. The time when independence of external sources of raw materials and markets counts most is in wartime. It is this fact which most people have in mind when they think of self-sufficiency as a national policy. For states lacking natural resources only the necessity of survival in war time would justify the immense cost in standards of living that would be necessary to achieve self-sufficiency.

Aside from the desire to be independent while engaged in war, self-sufficiency might be useful in the event of war between other states which resulted in a general disruption of international commerce. It might be desirable in order to shield the nation from having its economic life affected by events happening outside its boundaries. Finally, it might also be desirable in order to protect a nation from the effects of monopoly exploitation by another state controlling the sources of supply. But admitting that there are grounds for feelings of insecurity in connection with supplies of raw materials, a policy of national self-sufficiency does not seem to be the way to meet the situation. For most states the cost of achieving even a measure of self-sufficiency would far exceed any possible peace-time benefits gained by achieving independence of external disturbances. All economic life is subject to risks of disturbance, internal and external, but that is no reason for not engaging in it. It is far wiser to guard against such contingencies by appropriate international means than to deprive the nation of the immense advantages of trade over a wide area. This is true even of the countries comparatively well supplied with raw materials, such as the United States and Russia.

Furthermore, each nation which seeks self-sufficiency by national measures is interfering in some degree with the possibility of developing international trade in general. In this respect it is injuring not only itself but other nations as well. Hence the aim of self-sufficiency is incompatible with the notion of international economic life in general. It is accordingly very difficult to see how a claim for changing the status quo in order to make the claimant country more self-sufficient can properly be the subject of international procedures of peaceful change.

Ethnic Unity

Another aim of national policy which often calls for changes in the status quo is that of ethnic unity. The validity of this aim is more persuasive to the average man than those mentioned above because it is, at least on the surface, a peace-time aim. Presumably ethnic unity is sought for reasons of sentiment and in order to achieve more harmonious conditions in time of peace, and not to increase the war-time strength of the nation. Hence the aim is not in itself incompatible with the notion of international procedures of peaceful change.

But there are two almost insuperable difficulties which are encountered in claims of this character. The first one is that the peoples of Europe are, in many places, so inextricably mixed together that it would be practically out of the question to unite them on ethnic grounds by redrawing boundaries. Often several national groups will be found in one small area and it would be impossible to gratify the ethnic aspirations of one group without at the same time creating ethnic difficulties for the other groups. The second difficulty is that even though ethnic unity is sought wholly as a peace-time aim, it usually cannot be achieved through territorial revision without altering the relative power positions of the nations involved. Either the territory occupied by the minority is of strategic value, or the size of the minority is such as to have a definite effect on the man-power of the countries involved. Where this is the case it will make little difference that the purpose of seeking the change is wholly peaceful and without any reference to war-time strength. As indicated above, where considerations of national security enter in, they will be paramount to all others.

It is possible that in certain specific cases some degree of ethnic unity could be achieved by actual transfer of territory, provided adequate means of compensation could be devised and satisfactory guarantees given against upsetting the existing balance of power. But in the majority of cases no such solution seems possible. In these cases the most promising way to deal with the minorities problem would seem to be to develop more effective international machinery for protecting minorities. It often happens that the national groups of one country which find themselves within the boundaries of another would prefer to remain within the alien jurisdiction provided they are permitted to retain their cultural inheritance. Much of the difficulty with the existing international machinery for the protection of minorities is due to the fact that it does not represent a universal obligation imposed equally on all nations having minority groups within their borders, but is an obligation forced on certain states by the Allied Powers after the War. If all states, including the victorious Powers, accepted the obligation without discrimination and if more effective ways were devised for investigating conditions of minorities in all countries, much of the argument for transferring territory to achieve ethnic unity would be removed.

CHAPTER TWO

RAW MATERIALS

THE unevenness in the distribution of raw materials among the Great Powers is striking. Two of them, the United States and Soviet Russia, have an abundance of nearly everything necessary for modern industrial development. Two others, Great Britain and France, are fairly well off by reason of their extensive colonial empires. The other three, Germany, Japan and Italy, have no supplies at all of some of the most essential raw materials and are largely dependent on outside sources for others.

This differential provides the basis for the most insistent claims for alteration of the status quo. For many years, the nations less favorably situated have vigorously and repeatedly called attention to the need for greater equality in the distribution of raw materials. Deficiency in raw materials was an important factor in inspiring Japanese action in Manchuria and the Italian conquest of Ethiopia. Germany's dependence on outside sources is the ground most strongly urged in support of her claim for the return of her former colonies.

Before it is possible to assess the value of these claims, it is necessary to inquire why nations desire to have sources of raw materials within their own territory. Raw materials are things which are normally exploited by private enterprise for sale in the open market. Presumably anyone having the price can purchase such raw materials as he needs, regardless of his nationality. Mankind long ago invented numerous devices whereby economic transactions can be carried on across national boundaries. What special advantages, then, do nations seek from having raw material sources within their own political jurisdictions?

The possible advantages may be divided into two groups, those relating to the war-time strength of the nation and those relating to the peace-time economic needs of the people.[1] The importance of this distinction cannot be too strongly emphasized. The two aims are to a large extent incompatible. Things which increase the war potential of a nation often are a detriment to the economic welfare of its people in time of peace. Furthermore, from the standpoint of procedures of peaceful change, the distinction is decisive. To the extent that demands for a greater share in raw material sources are prompted by a desire to increase the war strength of the nation making the demands, they would seem to be outside the scope of procedures of peaceful change. For it is idle to expect that nations possessing an abundance of raw materials could be persuaded to give them up in order to increase the war potential of other nations. To the extent that

[1] Cf. Eugene Staley, *Raw Materials in Peace and War,* Chap. III.

a redistribution of raw material sources would serve to disturb the relative power positions of the parties concerned, it would be resisted by every possible means.

The distinction is particularly important because it is seldom openly made by governments seeking greater shares in the distribution of raw materials. It is very difficult to discover whether such demands are made on the basis of peace-time purposes or to increase the fighting strength of the claimant nation. Often the officials of the government making the demand do not themselves seem to know. Yet the determination of this point is crucial in deciding whether or not the demand can receive serious consideration.

It is probably true that in a majority of cases, although the fact is not openly stated, nations seeking to get sources of raw materials within their own jurisdiction are thinking of them chiefly in terms of the war-time strength of the nation. The power to win wars, and hence to direct the course of events in international affairs, rests in large part upon the ability to obtain raw materials as needed. Perhaps the most important element in the defeat of the Central Powers in the World War was the drying up of their supplies of essential raw materials and food stuffs. The revelation of the vital importance of raw materials in that war has aroused strong feelings of insecurity in countries that are dependent on outside sources for their raw materials. This has led in turn to an intense struggle on the part of the Great Powers to put themselves in an advantageous position regarding raw materials.

So long as the notion of "self-help" persists as the ultimate way of protecting or obtaining rights in the international sphere, nations will be greatly concerned over this matter of raw materials from the standpoint of war-time purposes. National security will seem to depend upon securing an adequate supply of raw materials of war. But this inevitably leads into an endless competition for raw materials similar to an armament race. For the only measure of an adequate supply of raw materials is one that will give superiority over any potential enemies. But the potential enemies are using the same measure, and all nations cannot be superior at the same time.

The need of adequate supplies for war purposes prompts the desire to have sources of supply within the national domain. Only in this manner is the danger of being cut off in war time avoided. Self-containment thus becomes the goal of national policy. But for most nations self-containment can only be purchased at an immense cost in peace-time standards of living. For some of them the choice between cannon and butter is real. Nevertheless, the ultimate possibility of war seems to demand that the sacrifice be made.

In connection with self-sufficiency, it is necessary to recall certain facts of economic geography and modern technology. Raw material sources are, it is true, widely distributed over the earth's surface, but they are not distributed in nicely assorted packages. A particular territory will have a large supply of one raw material but be wholly lacking in the other materials which are normally used with it in industry. A demand for self-sufficiency as regards sources of all raw materials essential for war purposes could be satisfied only through redistribution of whole continents or many small strips of territory. Even if the demand for control were limited to areas which produce the principal war materials, it would have to direct itself, not primarily at what is now colonial territory, but at the territories forming part of the home land of other states.

Furthermore, a claim for jurisdiction over raw material producing territory for purposes of increasing war strength by implication contains a claim for increased naval strength, unless the territory claimed is adjacent to the home land. Sovereignty over territory which produces raw materials is no guaranty of availability in war time. The latter depends not on title to territory, but on freedom of communications and therefore on naval supremacy.

To the extent that demands for access to raw materials are motivated by the desire to strengthen the military position of the nation, they are beyond the range of new procedures of peaceful change. So long as the security of nations is conceived of in terms of individual action, it is foolish to talk of devising peaceful procedures to enable some nations to get power advantages over other nations, or even to try to "equalize" fighting power by redistributing raw materials.

But aside from the question of the value of raw materials in war, the control over the sources of supply is, or can be, a vitally important matter in the economic relations of nations in peace time. With the increasing industrialization of nations, a steady supply of raw materials at reasonable prices is an essential part of the peace-time economy of most nations. Any outside agency that is in a position to control the flow of essential raw materials is in a position to do a considerable amount of harm to the economic life of nations which happen to be without sources of supply of their own. By demanding monopoly prices such an agency might disrupt the normal economic life of other nations and under certain conditions might even induce a lower standard of living.

No country which finds itself at the mercy of some other country for the supply of some raw materials necessary to its industrial life is going to be very happy over that dependency. It is all very well to say that those who possess sources of supply are anxious to sell, and that the problem is merely one of purchasing power. That is undoubtedly true under normal conditions, but the fact still remains that in certain situations the power to control exists, and can be used to obtain competitive advantage.

Under the existing organization of the international community there is nothing to prevent a nation having a supply of raw materials from making use of that supply in any way it sees fit. No international code of fair practices exists to limit its power to take advantage of other states less advantageously situated. It can permit and even encourage attempts at monopoly control on the part of its own producers. It can allow discrimination in favor of home consumers or manufacturers and against foreigners. It can permit the sudden cutting off of the supply of some essential commodity to another state resulting in the disruption of the industry of that state. There is no obligation to exploit the raw materials in a manner that is beneficial to the community at large, rather than to the state which happens to have the source of supply within its borders. States are as free in this respect as they are to disrupt foreign industries by the imposition of tariffs and other trade barriers.

In practice, many measures have been taken by those in control of sources of supply of raw materials which have operated as restrictions on the free marketing of the raw materials. These restrictive measures may be grouped under two general heads: (1) fiscal measures and trade barriers; and (2) production control schemes. Again, in the case of both these groups but especially the second, one may distinguish between the situations *(a)* where the source of the raw material is largely in one country and the exercise of sovereignty of that state will give it an effective monopoly position in the international community, and *(b)* where the source of the raw material is in a few states and an effective monopoly position requires the coöperation of those states or of the controlling groups within them.

Not all of the above measures have had an adverse effect on the interests of consumers. Moreover, many of the schemes which have sought monopolistic advantages have not been successful. Nevertheless, since the resort to devices of this kind causes nations without supplies of raw materials to have feelings of insecurity, it is necessary to take some note of the nature and effect of these devices. This is especially true since the tendency to resort to restrictive schemes seems to be increasing.[2]

Fiscal Measures and Trade Barriers

The first type of obstacle to access to raw materials customarily takes the form of export taxes, embargoes or other restrictions on exploitation, not for the purpose of increasing prices, but to raise rev-

[2]For a detailed consideration of these schemes, see Staley, *op. cit.*, Chaps. V, VI and VII.

enue, give home consumers an advantage over foreign consumers, conserve the supply for war purposes, encourage development of home processing industries, force exploitation by home capital and home labor, or similar aims. All such actions are based on the accepted notion that a country can do what it likes with the raw materials in its territories, regardless of the effect on foreign consumers.

The practice of levying export taxes seems to be confined largely to non-industrialized countries, and is resorted to mainly for raising revenue. The exploitation of a raw material which is exclusively exported is a tempting source of revenue. Often such taxes provide the only means whereby a state which possesses a quantity of raw material but lacks the capital and skill to exploit it can share in the profits. It frequently happens that raw materials in non-industrialized countries are exploited by foreign capital and exported without direct advantage to the local economy except in the payment of wages to local labor and the incidental purchase of supplies. This is apt to make the local inhabitants believe that they are being deprived of their rightful inheritance by foreigners. Such feelings may be counteracted to some extent by the exaction of sizable taxes on the exploitation and export of the material. Thus at one time one half of the total government revenues of Chile were derived from taxes on the mining and export of nitrates.

Such taxes for revenue purposes, where the tax-levying country has a virtual monopoly, undoubtedly increase the cost of the raw material to the consumer, but that does not mean that they are necessarily an obstacle to the access to the raw material in question by foreign countries. A League of Nations report on export duties found that "When moderate in amount and when levied on a product produced on a large scale and almost entirely exported, they may be said to be no more objectionable economically than any other form of taxation falling directly on production."[3] All taxes on production tend to divert trade from the channels it might otherwise take if left free, and to that extent might make such trade less profitable to the community as a whole. But that is true of many types of intervention which are nevertheless tolerated by the community because they are thought to serve some other purpose. It is quite possible that the power to levy export taxes might be abused to such an extent that foreign consumers were cut off from their supply of a particular raw material. But where the object of the tax is revenue for the government, it would obviously be foolish to fix the tax at a level which discouraged exploitation and hence reduced the amount of revenue received. In general, the ability

[3]*Export Duties,* League of Nations, Economic and Financial Section (Documentation of the International Economic Conference, Geneva, May, 1927), Introduction by Hipolit Gliwic, cited by Staley, *op. cit.,* p. 68.

to tax the exploitation of raw materials is not a serious threat to access to such raw materials by foreign users, so long as the object of the tax is revenue.

But government intervention in the exploitation of raw materials for export is for many purposes besides the raising of revenue. Sometimes discriminatory export duties are resorted to in order to force local processing or fabrication of the material in question. The same means are often used to favor national shipping or warehousing. Frequently governments intervene to force the use of native labor in the exploitation of raw materials, and occasionally to encourage the use of local capital. Such acts of intervention do not have as their object the efficient production and distribution of the material in question, but some other object which can usually be had only at the cost of efficient production. This type of intervention is generally on behalf of particular national groups who seek advantage in competition with foreign interests. As in the case of other types of intervention, if carried too far self-corrective elements are apt to come into play sooner or later.

Production Control Schemes

The second group of restrictions on access to raw materials consists of production control schemes.

Not many of these schemes have as their declared purpose the restriction of the market in order to force an artificially high level of prices. Efforts in this direction have not been generally successful. It is seldom that an agency or country will have such complete control over the sources of supply as to be able to maintain a monopoly price for any length of time. When an effort is made to do this, buyers cut their demands to the lowest possible level, encouragement is given to the use of substitute commodities and to synthetic production, sources of supply not previously exploited are opened for production. Often there is a lack of discipline among the parties to the scheme of monopolistic control, resulting in a failure to maintain the agreed price level. But in spite of the fact that such schemes are seldom successful over a period of time, the fact that they may be instituted at any time and may disrupt the industrial organization of consumer countries is bound to be a source of feelings of insecurity in consumer countries.

The customary type of production control scheme is not ostensibly for monopolistic purposes but is instituted in a falling market in order to protect producers from complete disorganization of the price scale. This has been true of practically all of the schemes initiated since the onset of the recent depression. Where there has in fact been a disastrous fall in prices, such schemes do not seem to arouse as much opposition among consumers as do outright monopoly practices. It is often recognized that measures taken to arrest drastic deflationary tendencies may operate for the benefit of the community as a whole as well as for the producers. The attempts that were made to adopt restriction schemes in sugar and in wheat in recent years did not arouse much consumer opposition because it was generally felt that decisive measures were necessary in order to restore orderly marketing conditions in these commodities.

But it often happens that schemes which begin innocently enough as emergency measures to meet a crisis turn into more or less permanent devices to protect the producer from the inconveniences of normal competition and to enable him to maintain an artificially high price level. The stabilization which was the aim of the original scheme is lost sight of in the natural desire of the producers to avoid as many of the risks of industrial life as possible, and to seek a constantly higher price level. Stabilization of prices, when left to producers, is almost always stabilization upward. This was well illustrated in the history of the Stevenson rubber restriction scheme. That scheme started innocently enough as an attempt to lift rubber prices up to the cost of production but as the plan met with success the approved level of prices kept moving upward.

The notable thing about all of these schemes is

that they are conceived and instituted in the interest of producers. Consumers ordinarily have no voice in the scheme. So far as the general welfare of the community is thought of, it is conceived to depend upon the welfare of the producers as a group. It is undoubtedly true that if, under a given set of conditions, even efficient producers in a particular industry cannot succeed in making a profit, the industry is bound to be disorganized and the whole community will suffer. Under such conditions price control through restriction of production may be of general benefit. But such price control can be a very powerful weapon under appropriate conditions, and the temptation is strong to use it for the exclusive benefit of the producers at the expense of the rest of the community.

This does not mean, however, that restrictive schemes should not be permitted under any circumstances, but merely that they should not be permitted to operate in the exclusive interest of one group. This is primarily a problem of representation. Up to the present time, only rarely has the consumer been permitted to participate in any way in the operation of restrictive schemes, and then only in an advisory capacity. If the community is to be protected against the misuse of this power, it is necessary that the consumer be represented along with the producer in the determination of policy. No one thought of consumer representation in the days of free competition, since presumably the consumer's interest was automatically protected by the operation of the free market. But all restrictive schemes interfere with that operation, and unless some other system of checks is substituted, there is considerable danger of exploitation. In the national field consumer representation is difficult because the consumer is seldom organized effectively, but in the field of international trade, because of the uneven distribution of raw materials, whole countries are apt to be identified with producer or consumer interests and to formulate their national policies accordingly.

The actual amount of damage that has been done to consumer interests by the operation of control schemes, export taxes and other forms of intervention in international trade in raw materials is probably less than might be imagined in view of the number of devices that have been tried out. Usually the full success of such schemes requires a greater degree of monopoly control than individual nations possess in the case of most raw materials. As suggested above, the consumer is not wholly without weapons to fight such measures. Buyers' strikes, retaliatory measures, the use of substitutes have often been enough to discourage attempts at restrictive measures.

On the other hand it cannot be denied that countries without raw materials *fear* that such schemes may at some future time so operate. It is true, furthermore, that no international mechanism exists today which operates as an effective check on the use of such systems for the exclusive advantage of producers and against the interest of consumers or the general public. Hence there exists a feeling of insecurity in consumer countries which leads them to seek changes in the status quo in the interests of a wider distribution of raw materials. Unless some assurance can be given against exploitation of the consumer by those who, by historical accident, happen to control the sources of supply, this will be a constant source of dissatisfaction with the status quo, and a possible temptation to seek changes by forceful measures. It is probable that the problem of raw materials will not be satisfactorily settled until some method is worked out for establishing an effective international code of fair practice as a protection to the general community in its needs for raw materials. Only this will remove the feeling of insecurity and dependence on the part of nations lacking raw materials and the temptation to seek an assured supply by territorial changes.

Purchasing Power and Foreign Exchange

It has often been asserted that the real obstacle to the acquisition of raw materials by the nations not possessing them is lack of the money with which to purchase them. Thus it is said that in the case of most raw materials there is an abundance, not a scarcity. What producers of raw materials most desire is to dispose of them at a profit. Control schemes have been developed because of glut, not scarcity. The only reason why foreigners should experience any difficulty in acquiring ample stocks of raw materials is because they have to pay for them in the currency of the producing country, which means that they must acquire the necessary exchange. But owing to the extensive disruption of the mechanism of foreign trade in recent years some countries find it difficult if not impossible to acquire this exchange.

This difficulty may arise out of policies pursued by the raw material importing country itself or from policies pursued by countries which purchase the manufactures of this country. Imports of raw materials are normally financed on foreign credit—either in the form of bank loans or by financing commercial paper—and these credits are repaid only from the proceeds of the sale in a foreign market of the goods manufactured from the raw material, or from the sale of other exports. If nations which are importers of raw materials suddenly shift the allocation of such raw materials from the use of export industries to the use of industries operating for local consumption, either in the form of public works or a greatly expanded armament program, the balance of payment will shift and the normal expectation of repayment out of future foreign sales will disappear. This will result in a stringency of foreign credits and an inability to maintain the level of foreign purchases of raw materials.

If the allocation is temporary and the return to normal is blocked by the inability to finance purchases of raw materials abroad rather than the inability to find foreign markets for the manufactured product, it would seem possible to set up an international procedure for financing the raw material purchases. Such a procedure will be suggested in the last chapter.

But the credit stringency may also be due to a doubt in the minds of potential foreign creditors that the importer of raw materials will really find access to foreign markets for the disposal of his manufactured goods. In other words, certain nations will not have access to raw materials abroad because of their inability to sell their surplus manufactures abroad, owing to the existence of trade barriers.

It is true that in the case of most raw materials, the available supplies are ample to fulfill current peace-time needs, if only the problem of distribution could be solved. It is also true that trade in general across national boundaries is obstructed by numerous barriers imposed by governments, such as tariffs, embargoes, exchange restrictions, discriminating duties, etc. The obvious conclusion would seem to be that the way to improve distribution is to remove these barriers.

This traditional analysis of the problem is undeniably sound as far as it goes, but it is very exasperating to those countries which are experiencing difficulty in acquiring the raw materials they need. Thus according to Dr. Schacht:

> A considerable school of opinion holds that all that is needed is to restore the international exchange of goods. Germany's share will thus be increased, and she will again be able to purchase raw materials. These are the people who are always talking of free trade and the lowering of tariff walls. Everybody agrees with them, but no one has yet succeeded in translating their ideals into reality.[4]

The customary explanation of the maintenance of trade barriers is economic nationalism. Unfortunately this term is currently being used in so many different senses that it is gradually losing its usefulness as a conveyor of meaning. To many people economic nationalism is the label applied to the behavior of governments in placing barriers to international trade for the purpose of aiding national interests. But it is quite common to hypostatize this label into a *cause* of the behavior described. Why do nations place barriers to international trade? *Because* of economic nationalism. Here economic nationalism becomes not the behavior itself, but some inner compulsion toward it. But no evi-

[4]Hjalmar Schacht, "Germany's Colonial Demands," *Foreign Affairs,* Vol. 15 (January, 1937), p. 230.

dence has been found to indicate that this compulsion is part of the physical equipment of the human race, as, for example the urge to eat when hungry or the urge toward sexual gratification. Rather it seems to be a program of action consciously arrived at by intellectual processes in order to meet certain conditions or accomplish certain objectives. Instead of excoriating it as some inner propensity toward sin, one might better seek to discover the conditions which give rise to it. In other words, tariffs, quotas, and similar barriers to trade are not themselves the cause of our economic troubles but are evidence of some deeper maladjustments in our socio-economic organization.

When looked at in this way, economic nationalism becomes a policy or doctrine for reaching certain specific ends. Thus Staley describes it as "the doctrine that it is the duty of the sovereign authority to aim solely at the welfare of its own adherents in disregard of the welfare of the rest of the world." Or to state it in another way, economic nationalism is the belief that national economic welfare is best served by seeking national advantage directly rather than through the development of international economic life, and this concept of national economic interest is arrived at in many cases by identifying the interests of special groups with the interests of the nation.

Most schools of thought recognize that national

governments must seek the welfare of their own nations rather than that of some other. But some argue that this can best be achieved by regarding the nation as part of a larger economic system, upon the general health of which the welfare of the particular unit depends in large part. Others argue that the national economic welfare is something which can and should be treated as an independent thing, quite apart from the economic life of other nations, and that the more it is kept separate from other nations the better for the national economic welfare. This latter school may readily concede the benefits to be derived from specialization, but they argue that international life is subject to constant stresses and strains and that it is dangerous to place the national welfare at the mercy of these far-reaching external conditions over which the national government can have little if any control.

This is not the place to seek to settle this complicated issue. One can merely note that, so far as raw materials are concerned, our current industrial development seems to be unavoidably international. This is due to the wide variety of raw materials required in modern industrial civilization and to the fact that these materials are so unevenly distributed over the face of the earth without any regard for national boundaries. Two or three states are so situated that they might be able to get along without relying on outside supplies, but this would entail some hardship and lowering of living standards even for them, and the price seems too great to pay for the freedom from possible disturbances from outside sources. For other countries not so well situated a policy of self-sufficiency seems quixotic so long as there is any workable alternative.

Admitting the dangers involved in international trade, the alternatives appear to be far more threatening to the national welfare of industrialized states. It seems clear that the raw material needs of such nations cannot be supplied by any possible reshuffling of territories containing sources of supply. These sources are too concentrated to permit of division among the states of the world. On the other hand, efforts at self-sufficiency are costly and for most nations futile. The only possibility for economic health for most nations would seem to be a revival of world trade and a reintegration of all industrial nations into that trade.

The real problem is whether international trade is to be restored as an automatic system by the removal of governmental intervention, or whether it is to be subject to a large amount of governmental control. The problem is not whether the nations of the world will trade with each other at all. They are bound to trade or to revert to primitivism. The real problem is how this trade shall be conducted. In other words, what rôle will the governments of the world play in that trade?

The easiest thing to argue for is a reversion to the ideal of free trade and the removal of all government intervention. If nations are suffering from lack of trade and trade is stopped by state-made obstacles at the boundaries, then a simple solution would be to remove these obstacles. Thus it is often urged that the relative prosperity of the United States is not due to its protective tariff system but to the fact that internally it represents a wide trading area without barriers. If the other nations of the world would remove their trade barriers they would enjoy equal prosperity.

It is hardly worth while inquiring whether this position is valid, since there is little possibility that the nations of the world will adopt a policy of free trade within the foreseeable future. Behind the trade barriers of all nations vested interests have sprung up which would firmly resist any such move. Once industry has been allowed to develop behind a tariff wall, it is doubtless true that to remove the wall suddenly would be disastrous. In any event, the rigors of the automatic price system have proved to be such that governments show little disposition to expose their peoples to it without some protection. The cyclical depressions which are associated with the automatic system have grown to be so great in size and extent that nearly all governments have been forced into a more or less active rôle to alleviate their effects. The changing relations between government and industry which have become manifest in nearly every country to some extent will doubtless continue to make themselves felt in foreign trade and cannot be expected to stop at the boundaries.

On the other hand, the opposite extreme of an internationally planned economy seems an even more remote possibility. There are no signs of any disposition on the part of any considerable portion of the human society to delegate authority in the regulation of industry to some international agency. Even if the disposition existed, the techniques and skills necessary to handle such a colossal undertaking are probably lacking. For planning of this sort could not be partial but would have to be universal, with definite authority in the central organization to override conflicting national interests.

The most that can be hoped for at the present time seems to be a slow and cautious movement toward the revival of the system of international trade, but with government action playing a much larger rôle than formerly. The important thing is to know how this government intervention will be used. If the object of such action should be merely to gain competitive advantage for the nation as an independent economic unit, then there is little or no chance that a healthy international economic life can be reëstablished. But if the intervention of individual governments is motivated by the desire to increase international trade in general, there is some hope that a workable system can be evolved. However, a preliminary requirement would seem to be that some improvement should be made in the existing international machinery for the coördination of national economic policies. This subject will be touched upon later.

According to Dr. Schacht, the reason why it has not been possible to resume international trade through a general lowering of tariffs is that the economic strength of nations has become a vitally important factor in power politics.

> Today the possession of raw materials has become a political factor, just as the voluntary change of the currency standard has become a political instrument. People think that by withholding or sharing raw materials the political situation of a political opponent or friend can be correspondingly influenced.[5]

For this reason, says Dr. Schacht, nations situated as are Germany and Italy must strive to free themselves from dependence on outside sources.

> For any nation to live at the mercy of another is a complete impossibility. . . . A great nation that sees itself exposed to such a danger will employ all its powers to avoid it.

Hence governments, according to Dr. Schacht, are forced to intervene in commercial relations in order to protect the position of the nation in world politics.

[5] *Foreign Affairs,* Vol. 15, p. 230.

It is difficult to break into this vicious circle. Nevertheless, a way must be found if the system of international trade is to be successfully revived. A beginning might be made by the adoption of genuine open-door policies with respect to the exploitation of raw materials everywhere. These policies should be incorporated in international agreements because otherwise they would be subject to frequent change and would instill no confidence in other states. Eventually it might be possible to establish a system of international supervision of the operation of these agreements in order to give assurance that they were being carried out in good faith. But real progress cannot be expected until some means can be found to lessen the feelings of insecurity which now cause nations to subordinate everything to the building up of national power.

CHAPTER THREE

POPULATION PRESSURE

ONE of the most effective grounds on which to base claims for changes in the status quo is that of "overpopulation." Much has been heard in recent years about overcrowding in certain countries, threatening to lead to excessive hardship and even mass starvation unless relieved by territorial expansion. The action of Japan in causing Manchuria to be separated from China has been most often justified on this ground, as has Italy's Ethiopian adventure. "Overpopulation" has likewise been vigorously advanced as a basis for Germany's demands for the return of her colonies, and there are indications that Poland may be preparing to present certain demands for alteration of the status quo on the same ground. Overcrowding is a notion that is easily grasped by the man on the street and is apt to meet with a sympathetic response from him. Hence, it is a useful ground for gaining popular support for proposals for territorial revision.

As a basis for peaceful change, overpopulation immediately raises two questions: first, does any country in fact suffer from excess population? and second, if so, is it a condition that can be relieved by territorial revision or other types of peaceful change?

Overpopulation and Underpopulation

The answer to the first question requires some agreement on a test for the condition of overpopulation. Clearly there is no absolute test in the sense of there being in any one country more people than can be kept alive by the available means of subsistence. The mere fact of being alive is a denial of this test. But on the other hand, to deny that overcrowding ever exists seems equally untenable. One need only observe the immense physical labor that the people of some countries have to expend merely to extract the barest subsistence from the soil—countries in which a single poor crop may result in widespread famine and misery. Not only is there a great disparity in the pressure of the population against available resources, but there is a widespread realization of this disparity. In some agricultural countries one observes excessively long hours of toil, extreme frugality, cautious avoidance of waste, all this yielding a pitifully low standard of living. In other countries one finds relatively short hours of labor, extensive use of mechanical aids in place of physical exertion, wasteful methods of land utilization, coupled with high living standards and frequent opportunities for diversion. It is reasonable to account for this great disparity in living conditions to some extent at least on the ground, that in certain places there are too many people pressing against the available resources.

The most popular method of indicating population pressure is to cite statistics of simple density, such as the number of people per square mile of territory, or the number per square mile of arable land. The latter figures are often used to support the theory of the "Haves" and the "Have-nots" since they seem to show a very wide disparity as among the Great Powers. According to these figures the favored countries are Soviet Russia with 66 people per square mile of arable land, the United States with 100, and France with 294. Compared with these countries the so-called Have-nots are apparently very badly off. Thus Italy has 477, Germany 578, and Japan 2,418. The implication is that these latter countries are clearly suffering from overpopulation.

However, these density figures really have little, if any, value in indicating population pressure. Thus while Italy and Germany are clearly worse off than the United States and Soviet Russia, they are better off in this respect than a number of other countries which do not make demands for relief from population pressure. The countries (other than Japan) with a higher density per square mile of arable land than either Italy or Germany or China, Czechoslovakia, Austria, the Netherlands, India, England and Wales, Belgium, Egypt and Greece. A few of these, to be sure, have colonial empires, but the majority have not. Less than half of them are industrialized countries.

How misleading these density statistics sometimes are is indicated in the following table comparing the number of inhabitants per square kilometer in certain countries with the number of agrarian inhabitants per square kilometer of cultivated land.[1]

Country	*Total number of inhabitants per square kilometer*	*Number of agrarian inhabitants per square kilometer cultivated land*
France	74	35
England	195	83
Germany	137	91
Belgium	263	98
Netherlands	237	168
China	111	360

According to the first column of figures, China is very much better off in the manner of density than any of the countries mentioned except France, but according to the second column her agrarian density exceeds the most densely populated European countries by more than 100 per cent.

These figures likewise suggest the necessity for distinguishing between population pressure in terms of national economy, *i.e.,* roughly in terms of local food supply, and population pressure in terms of the relation between national economy and world economy, *i.e.,* the degree to which foodstuffs are

[1]Taken from Memorandum by M. F. Van Heek on "The Calculation of Population Pressure in Agrarian Territories inclined to be Self-Supporting," submitted to the General Study Conference on Peaceful Change.

imported. Thus the figures show that in France there are 39 non-agrarians to every kilometer of cultivated land, whereas in Belgium there are 165, indicating the relatively greater degree of Belgium's dependence on external sources of foodstuffs.

It is also clear that different peoples have different habits, and conditions which would seem to represent overcrowding to one nation would not seem so to another. Climatic conditions, degrees of industrialization, dietary habits all enter into the question. Thus while the statistics indicate that Japan has a very high density per square mile of arable land, it must be borne in mind that sea food plays a far larger part in the diet of the Japanese people than it does in that of any western country.

It is sometimes said that death rates are an accurate indication of standards of living and hence of population pressure—the higher the death rate the greater the pressure. In support of this position it is pointed out that death rates range from about 9 per 1,000 in New Zealand and Australia to 11 to 13 in Western Europe and America, to 16 to 19 in Eastern Europe and Japan, and above 25 in India and Egypt. But clearly these death rates are not directly reflected in *felt* population pressure, leading to demands for changes in the status quo. The countries with really high death rates, such as India, Ceylon and Egypt, do not seek to obtain relief through territorial expansion. What makes people feel population pressure, apparently, is not a low standard of living in itself but the degree to which they are aware that under changed conditions this low standard could be alleviated.[2]

Carr-Saunders has pointed out that a real condition of overpopulation would so weaken a country that it would probably be unable to make effective demands for relief.[3] One does not, for example, hear complaints of overpopulation and demands for new territory from China, although in this country the ratio of population to available resources is such as to induce an extremely low standard of living as compared with European countries.

It has been suggested the nations which are actually conscious of population pressure and which make demands for relief are those which are industrializing rapidly. They are not so much concerned about present conditions of overpopulation as they are about the rate of growth of population which seems to indicate that unless further room for expansion is made available their rate of improvement of living standards will slow down. The situation is similar to that found in the field of labor, where the demands for improved conditions come generally, not from the most poorly paid unorganized class of laborers, but rather from those who

[2]Cf. Warren S. Thompson, *Population Problems* (New York, 1930), pp. 370-1; *Danger Spots in World Population* (New York, 1929), pp. 14-15, 68-69.

[3]A. M. Carr-Saunders, *World Population* (Oxford, 1936), p. 324.

already have achieved a fairly decent standard of living and have a sufficient surplus to enable them to organize to enforce their demands. Only those who see the definite possibility of improving their condition by struggle will be apt to feel their existing condition strongly and seek to do something about it.

According to this view, the nations which would feel population pressure most are those which have already succeeded in achieving a moderately good standard of living and can see opportunities for increasing this standard in the future if only they can be assured of the resources on which to expend their capacities. Thus it is suggested that the middle death rate nations, those having death rates between 15 and 20, are apt to feel population pressure most. However, an inspection of the death rates of the various countries does not seem to bear this out. The figures mentioned are crude death rates. Kuczynski's table of yearly crude death rates of European countries from 1841 to 1933 gives the rates for the latter year as follows:[4]

Belgium	13.2	England & Wales	12.3
Switzerland	11.4	Bulgaria	15.4
Czechoslovakia	13.7	Portugal	17.6
Poland	14.2	Rumania	18.7
Germany	11.2	European Russia (1929)	19.5
Italy	13.7	Spain	16.4
France	15.8	Yugoslavia	19.2

[4]Robert R. Kuczynski, *The Measurement of Population Growth* (New York, 1936), pp. 162-163.

According to these figures the countries which should really "feel" population pressure are France, Bulgaria, Portugal, Rumania, Russia, Spain and Yugoslavia. But not Germany nor Italy.

It is possible that the "true" death rates of the various countries might accord more with this theory than the crude death rates which are used in this connection. Kuczynski has figured out these "true" rates for some countries at various dates. Unfortunately, he has not published such figures for eastern European or Asiatic countries. The following table shows these "true" rates for a few countries:[5]

Country	Years	Rate	Country	Years	Rate
England & Wales	(1920-22)	17.38	England & Wales	(1933)	16.45
France	(1920-3)	18.5	Scotland	(1930-32)	17.3
Germany	(1924-26)	17.44	Denmark	(1926-30)	16.2
Switzerland	(1920-21)	17.9	Norway	(1921/2-30/31)	16.03
Italy	(1921-22)	20.0	Sweden	(1926-30)	16.1
Australia	(1920-22)	16.35	Italy	(1930-32)	18.22
New Zealand	(1921-22)	15.61	New Zealand	(1933)	14.70

In this table the French death rate is much closer to that of its neighboring western European states than was the crude death rate. Italy's rate is apparently a little higher than that of the northern and western countries. It is possible that these figures combined with figures for eastern Europe and Asia might support the above-mentioned theory. But in any case the clamor over population pressure

[5]Kuczynski, *op. cit.*, pp. 184-187.

comes from certain specific countries and not from the whole group of countries with similar death rates. It seems plain that the standard of living, at least as reflected in relative death rates, is not in itself an explanation of *felt* population pressure, but must be accompanied by some other psychological factors.

Aspirations toward a bigger place in the sun or toward increased prestige undoubtedly serve as factors in felt population pressure. Nations which are growing rapidly usually expect the process to continue indefinitely and tend to picture themselves as requiring an increasingly important place in world affairs. This is often accompanied by a tendency to hurry the process by increasing the rate of growth of the population, so that other nations will be impressed not only with the needs but especially with the man-power of the nation seeking expansion. Everyone is familiar with the paradox that nations which complain loudest of population pressure are often the ones which work hardest to increase the size of their populations.[6] Or a nation may be seized by a fear of depopulation and seek to overcome the condition by moves to enhance its position in the world, as did France between 1880 and 1900. Or again, a nation may be suffering from a feeling of humiliation as a result of having been defeated in

[6]It is to be noted that so far the efforts in this direction do not seem to be meeting with success. Thus both Italy and Germany show a declining birth rate.

a war and forced to accept peace terms that reduce its importance in world affairs. Any one of these things when accompanied by a relatively high ratio of population to resources is apt to give rise to feelings of population pressure and demands for room for expansion.

There is reason to believe that Germany's claims for territorial revision to relieve her population pressure are based at least in part on feelings of this character. Thus Herr Hitler has stated Germany's case as follows:

> The duty of the foreign policy of a national State is to ensure the existence of the race included in that State by keeping a natural and healthy proportion between the numbers and the increase of the nation and the size and quality of the land in which they dwell.
>
> Nothing but sufficient space on the earth ensures freedom of existence to a nation. In this way only can the German nation defend itself as a world Power. For nearly two thousand years our national interests, as our more or less happily conceived foreign activities may be termed, played their part in the world's history. We ourselves can witness to that. For the great struggle of the nations from 1914 to 1918 was but the German nation struggling for its existence in the world, and it went by the name of the World War.
>
> At that time the German nation was ostensibly a world Power. I say "ostensibly", because it was really not a world Power. If the German nation had preserved the proportion I referred to above, Germany would really have been a world Power, and the War might, apart from all other factors, have ended in our favor.

Today Germany is not a world Power. From a purely territorial point of view, the area of the German Reich is insignificant compared with those of the so-called world Powers. England is not an example to be quoted, since the British Mother country is really but the great capital city of the British world Empire, which claims nearly a quarter of the earth's surface as its property. We must rather look at giant States such as the American Union, then at Russia and China—enclosed areas, some of them ten times as big as the German Empire. France herself must be reckoned as one of their number. She is constantly adding to her army from the colored populations of her immense Empire. If France goes on as she is now doing for three hundred years, she will have a powerful enclosed territory from the Rhine to the Congo, filled with a race continually becoming more and more bastardized. That is where French colonial policy differs from Germany's former one.

Ours neither increased the lands occupied by the German race, nor did it make the criminal attempt to strengthen the Empire by introducing black blood. The Askari in German East Africa were a small, hesitating step in that direction, but actually they were only used for defence of the colony itself.

We have ceased to enjoy any position compared with the other great States of the world, and that thanks merely to the fatal direction of our nation in foreign policy, to absolute lack of any tradition, as I might call it, of a definite policy in foreign affairs, and to loss of all sound instinct and urge to maintain ourselves as a nation.

All this must be remedied by the National-Socialist movement, which must attempt to remove the disproportion between our population and our area—the latter seen both as the source of nourishment and the basis of political power

—between our historic past and the hopelessness of our present impotence.[7]

But to the extent that population pressure is related to power considerations, it seems to be beyond the range of procedures of peaceful change. Nations cannot be expected to agree voluntarily to a change in the status quo which enhances the claimant nation's power and influence in world affairs at the expense of others, and there is no use in trying to invent procedures to induce them to do so, unless of course such procedures should be backed by community pressure. But no basis for community coercion seems to be present in cases of this kind.

Aside from claims involved in power politics, there are undoubtedly instances of felt population pressure legitimately based on conditions of overcrowding. The patent disparity among the nations in the amount of land and resources in relation to population is a continuing source of unrest, and is bound to lead to agitation for alterations in the status quo. Granting that this is so, the question remains whether there are any international remedies, such as transfer of territory or migration,

[7]Adolph Hitler, *My Battle* (Boston, 1933), pp. 275-277. Unless the proposed expansion is to take place on land now uninhabited, the above program would seem to imply that the native population of any land claimed by Germany would have to be removed or exterminated. For how else would it be possible to establish the "natural and healthy proportion between the numbers and the increase of the nation and the size and quality of the land in which they dwell"?

or whether it is a condition that must be left to local measures.

Industrialized Countries

In industrialized countries, population pressure may be caused for a time by industrial depression or by the restriction of opportunities for foreign trade, but this is different from the population pressure that is encountered in agricultural countries. The former, according to Carr-Saunders, is due, not to excessive growth of population, but to a recession of conditions leaving the population stranded.[8] In this situation, a restoration of the conditions offers a possible and rapid remedy, whereas in the case of the overcrowded agricultural country the probabilities are that the former condition can only be restored by the slow process of reducing the size of the population.

It has often been pointed out that unemployment is not a test of overpopulation, and this has been borne out by the case of the United States. It is even conceivable that an appreciable increase in the size of the population, if of the right kind, would *reduce* unemployment in a particular country rather than add to it. Population pressure in industrialized countries is attributable more to maladjustments in the economic system than to increase of population. As a matter of fact, the problem of overcrowding

[8] Carr-Saunders, *op. cit.*, pp. 139-40.

in industrialized countries may be a regional problem rather than one of national extent. In the United States, for example, one finds a wide range of conditions running from excessive overcrowding to clear signs of underpopulation. Practically all of the possible population problems are here reproduced within the limits of one country.

Thus we find a number of distinct groups which are clearly suffering from pressure of population on resources although there is no insufficiency of gross natural resources of the nation. The existence of these groups is due, not to shortage in territory or raw materials but to maladjustments of the economic system which isolate them from social contact and from access to adequate economic opportunity. It is possible to identify at least six large rural groups in the United States, comprising in all some 20,000,000 people who are forced by lack of available resources to live at a marginal or bare subsistence level, although the country as a whole may be said to be underpopulated.[9]

[9]These groups are, roughly, the Appalachian and Ozark Mountain groups comprising together around 5,000,000; about 800,000 rural people in the white pine cut-over regions of Michigan, Minnesota, and Wisconsin; the marginal cotton workers in the Southeastern and Southwestern states, a large proportion tenants and share croppers, with their families, numbering about 12,000,000 people; part of the people in the winter wheat area of the southern great Plains region, about 1,100,000, in which recurrent drought and soil inadequacy apparently offer insuperable difficulties to much of the farming; and a similar group of about 800,000 people in the spring wheat area to the north. (*Six Rural Problem Areas,* Research Monograph 1, Rural Research Unit, Federal Emergency Relief Administration, 1935.)

In addition, in all of the larger cities there are large numbers of unskilled marginal workers who exist at a bare subsistence level on part-time work or on government relief funds. Likewise there are large numbers of marginal workers in the coal mining industry who cannot be expected to find adequate employment in that industry under any conditions now foreseeable and who eke out a precarious existence "bootlegging" coal and in subsistence farming. These people do not have the resources to move to new regions nor the training to find other employment.

It is perfectly true that these people are unable to obtain an adequate living standard out of the resources actually available to them. Not only do they themselves suffer from this fact, but they are a serious burden on the remaining population. Yet it cannot be said that there is a total shortage of resources for the country at large. Even with present techniques there is ample farm land in the United States to feed a larger population than now exists in this country. Vast supplies of raw material are available for a much higher rate of industrial production than now exists. In other words, the available physical resources are ample to provide a high standard of living for more people than now live in this country. Yet about a fifth of the present population find the land and resources available to them inadequate for anything but a bare subsistence standard of living. These people unquestionably suffer from overcrowding, although the country as a whole is probably underpopulated.

Likewise in Great Britain a serious problem exists in the so-called depressed areas representing communities which have become stranded as a result of changing economic and social conditions. There seems to be no probability that the people in these areas will be able to work out a satisfactory living from the resources actually available, yet the population of Great Britain as a whole enjoys a high standard of living and the country is not regarded as overcrowded. The same situation is doubtless true in other industrialized countries of Europe. If a stranded community or class is large enough or vocal enough, it can create a definite impression of overcrowding, although the total resources of the country are more than ample for the total population. The tests that have been devised to show overpopulation in industrial countries such as high death rate, low real income, etc., do not in fact reveal conditions of overpopulation in the industrial countries of Europe. Yet in many countries there are extensive groups pressing hard against available resources, and these groups give all the appearance of overcrowding.

What makes these marginal groups especially important is the fact that their birth rate is invariably much higher than that of the country as a whole and that they are reproducing at a rate above that required for their replacement. Furthermore, in each group the highest birth rate is found among the families which are below the average of their own group in intelligence.[10] At the same time the more highly educated half of the population are reproducing at a rate substantially below replacement. It is also probably true that, both in the United States and in England, those persons in the stranded areas and marginal groups who had capacity and energy managed in some manner to escape from the group, leaving behind those of lesser capacity. The fact that these people are reproducing much faster than the more capable part of the population is a matter of considerable significance in connection with the cultural and genetic inheritance of the nation. It might also create the paradoxical situation that, even though the total population of the country was decreasing, the population pressure of these marginal groups would be increasing.

In regard to industrial countries, then, signs of overcrowding in various areas cannot be taken as indicating overpopulation for the country as a whole. The probabilities are that the pressure represents marginal groups that have become stranded by changing economic conditions. The way to meet situations of this kind, so far as they can be met at

[10]Cf. Frank Lorimer and Frederick Osborn, *Dynamics of Population* (New York, 1934), pp. 193-5.

all, would seem to be by adjustments in the socio-economic structure.

In any event it does not seem that such problems could be solved either by transfer of territory or by migration to foreign soil. So far as the former is concerned, the experience of the United States is a pretty clear indication that the difficulty is not the lack of available land. Whether such land is within the national domain or under a foreign flag, the cost of moving inhabitants of stranded or depressed areas to it and getting them established successfully appears in most cases to be prohibitive. This is especially true since the inhabitants of such areas usually belong in the lower capacity groups of the population, and it would require an extra amount of effort to establish them either in a new place or a new vocation. The same effort spent in readjusting the socio-economic system in order to bring the stranded areas back into it would undoubtedly show far greater results. In any event it is too much to expect that countries with available land would let down their immigration barriers to immigrants of this type, since the primary motive in establishing these barriers was to keep such people out. There is little to be gained from any viewpoint in taking people from a stranded area in one country and setting them up in a new stranded area in another country.

Agricultural Countries

In the case of the agricultural countries the problem is somewhat different. Here the cause of overcrowding may usually be traced to growth of population rather than changing economic conditions. Hence the manner of handling it must be different. The possibilities which suggest themselves are (1) improved techniques of land utilization, (2) industrialization, (3) limiting the growth of the population, (4) migration or the transfer of territory.

There is no reason to suppose that agricultural techniques will not be constantly improved. But the process is slow and is not likely to show much effect on overcrowding in agricultural countries for many years. Furthermore, new methods of land utilization usually call for capital outlay on a substantial scale, which places them beyond the reach of those suffering from overcrowded conditions in agricultural areas.

Industrialization has worked in several instances, notably in Japan, but it depends primarily on four things: (1) an adequate supply of raw materials, (2) markets, (3) capital savings, and (4) capacity for acquiring technical skill. Where any or all of these things are lacking it is possible that they may be made up from outside sources, but this would normally presuppose a resumption of the system of international trade on a wide scale. It would mean, for example, that part of the existing agrarian population or the increment to the population would have to live on imported foodstuffs. In any case, industrialization would be a comparatively slow method of taking care of surplus population.

Limiting the growth of the population means simply birth control. If the government of a particular country had the power to determine which members of the population should have children and how many, it is undoubtedly true that overcrowding could eventually be controlled. But people are not generally willing to entrust this power to political governments. Where the matter is left to the people themselves, certain groups of the population will resort to birth control much more readily than others.

Generally speaking, these are urban groups engaged in industrial pursuits. Rural groups tend to maintain a high birth rate even in the face of adverse economic conditions. Hence there is little reason to suppose that the dissemination of birth control information will have a very marked effect on surplus population in agricultural countries for many years to come.

Reduction in the birth rate would, when achieved, undeniably lead to a positive reduction of population pressure. It is true that it would not solve the problem of finding employment for the generation now ready to go to work, but it would, within approximately fifteen years, considerably change the proportion between producers and consumers.

The next possibility is that overcrowding in agricultural countries might be relieved by emigration to foreign soil. It is true, of course, that if there are too many people in a country, one way to relieve the pressure is to remove some of them from the country. However, there are several difficulties connected with migration as a remedy of overcrowding. In the first place it would only offer permanent relief in a country of stationary population. But such countries are not apt to feel population pressure. In the case of countries of increasing population, the relief would only be temporary, unless migration could be kept up at a high rate.

Take for example the case of Poland, an agricultural country with increasing population pressure. While a decline in the birth rate seems to have been in progress here[11] as in the countries of western Europe, the net reproduction rate in 1927 was still as high as 1.3.[12] At this rate the population is increasing every generation by 30 per cent. In order to prevent Poland's existing population pressure from increasing, it would be necessary for 30 per cent of her population to migrate each generation. It is possible that places could be found in other countries for this number of Polish emigrants for

[11]Carr-Saunders, *op. cit.*, p. 124.

[12]Robert R. Kuczynski, "The Decline in Fertility," *Economica*, May, 1935.

some time to come, but it is highly doubtful that emigration on such a scale could be kept up indefinitely. Apparently the only permanent solution of a population problem of this kind is a further considerable decline in the birth rate. But it cannot be hoped that the situation will be substantially relieved in this manner for years to come.

But granted that migration would bring at least temporary relief from population pressure in certain cases, there are still many difficulties with it. The problem of costs has already been mentioned. The least expensive type of migration is to areas of highly developed industrial activity, where jobs are ready to absorb the immigrants. But if the migration is to underdeveloped regions, even for purposes of starting an agricultural economy, it must be accompanied by considerable capital investment. Obviously this capital cannot come from the underdeveloped region. It must either be furnished by the emigrant state or be made available by foreign loans.

Another difficulty arises out of the type of emigrant to be selected. Only certain kinds of migration would be helpful, others would be definitely harmful to overcrowded agricultural countries like Poland. The class of population which these countries could most readily spare are the uneducated rural agricultural workers and unskilled laborers. Yet these are the people who would need the most help in getting started in other countries, and who are usually not wanted in underpopulated countries. The sort of people who would have the initiative and courage to migrate are the kind the overcrowded countries most need at home.

In other words, the only kind of migration which would help the overpopulated states is controlled migration and not the individual unselected migration of the past. It is probably true that there are certain underpopulated countries which can take the kind of people the overpopulated countries can afford to let go. However, this can scarcely be left to the free play of chance, *i.e.*, to unrestricted immigration, but must be handled by direct agreement between governments. A beginning has been made in this direction in the treaties Poland has signed with France and other nations governing temporary and permanent migration.[13] In these treaties the receiving country specifies the kind and number of immigrants it wants and the sending country is able to specify the conditions under which the migration will be carried out.

Most of the present restrictions on immigration were imposed at a time when populations were still growing rapidly. These restrictions were to some extent motivated by the belief that the "natural increase" of the country was sufficient to provide for a healthy growth of the population, and further

[13]For details, see Carr-Saunders, *op. cit.*, pp. 150-153.

increase by immigration would bring about overcrowding. There was also the belief that the kind of immigrants who were coming in were of the lowest quality, and that since they would work for low wages, they would defeat the efforts of organized labor to improve conditions of labor.

The rather remarkable recent trend of population statistics forecasting a definite decline in the population has apparently not yet penetrated the minds of the public. When it is finally realized that the present trend is downward and that the rate of decline may grow sharply greater, there may be a definite reversal of opinion regarding the desirability of immigration. It is quite possible that when the full significance of the trend toward small families is brought home to the public, a competition for desirable aliens will replace the present trend toward exclusion. If, for example, the British public should come to realize that at the present low fertility rate the population would be reduced to half its current size within a century, that would undoubtedly have repercussions on their immigration policy. But at least until there is widespread comprehension of the implications of present population trends, one may predict that, regardless of the needs of certain countries, there will be no general lowering of existing barriers to individual immigration, and that the only migration of any size will be selective migration conducted under agreements between governments.

This leaves the question whether transfer of territory can serve to relieve the overcrowding of agricultural countries. On the basis of past experience with expansion, there is little to support the assumption that surplus population flows readily to overseas possessions or colonies. In fact, according to Grover Clark, the evidence against it is "devastatingly clear."[14] Thus it is shown that in 1931, there were less than half as many Europeans of all nationalities in all the Italian colonies as there were Italians on the Island of Manhattan in New York City. In 1913, twenty years after Germany got most of her colonies, less than 20,000 Germans had emigrated permanently to the German colonies.[15]

It is not safe to conclude from these figures, however, that colonies would not under existing conditions be of any value in relieving the population of some countries. It must be recalled that when the above records were made, immigration was freely permitted in the countries of the new world. From the standpoint of climate, natural resources, economic opportunities and social position, these countries offered far greater attractions to settlers than did available colonies in Africa. Had the same restrictions on immigration now existing in the United States and the British Dominions been in existence at the time these statistics were gathered,

[14]Grover Clark, *The Balance Sheets of Imperialism* (New York, 1936), p. 9.

[15]*Ibid.*, p. 10.

it is fair to assume that the record of migration to colonies from countries feeling population pressure might have been somewhat different.

An important factor is climate. While it is true that many people from temperate zones have difficulty in adjusting themselves to tropical conditions, it has not been established that such adjustment is impossible. Constant improvement in medical science and sanitation and mechanical advances in refrigeration and the supplanting of physical labor by machines have steadily improved the possibilities of migration to tropical countries by people from the temperate zones. However, it is still true that a much greater effort is required to settle emigrants from European countries in tropical or semitropical areas than in countries with a climate similar to their own. As long as migration to temperate zones was possible, there was no particular reason to make this effort. But now that the temperate zones are practically closed to migration on a large scale, there is more reason to make the effort to settle in the less desirable zones.

There is the feeling, of course, that internal migration, no matter how distant, does not result in a loss of the emigrants from the population, whereas those who migrate to foreign jurisdictions are apt to be permanently lost to the fatherland. This is to a large extent true. Receiving nations generally endeavor to nationalize immigrants and to assimilate them as a permanent part of the population. The nation of the emigrant, on the other hand, does not like to lose all hold over him, especially if he is still capable of rendering military service to the state. Hence the strong desire to provide land under the flag on which the surplus population can settle.

One possible way of lessening this desire would be to provide more adequate safeguards for immigrant minorities. If nations were prepared to permit immigrants to retain their nationality and not to try to assimilate them against their will, the countries from which they migrated might not be so concerned to have them under their own protection. If, as suggested above, migration in the future is to be conducted under treaty arrangements, such matters as this might well be included in the terms of the agreement. The advantages of such an arrangement would necessarily have to be weighed against the problems which it might introduce for the country of immigration.

In brief, it does not seem safe to conclude that, because there has been little movement from certain countries to their colonies in the past, there never would be such movement on an appreciable scale in the future. The conditions affecting population movements today are quite different from what they were formerly. It is probably unwise, for example, to conclude that Italian settlement of Ethiopia will resemble in any way the past record of Italian colonization in other north African possessions. But the fact remains that the only type of territory which could conceivably be transferred to overcrowded countries is the so-called backward areas, now occupied by populations accustomed to an even lower standard of living than that found in the overcrowded agricultural countries of Europe. Before such lands could be made to support large numbers of immigrants on a higher scale of living than that enjoyed by the natives, it would be necessary to alter the entire economy of the territory. This would be an immense task and it is highly doubtful that an agricultural country suffering from overcrowding would have the resources to undertake it.

There remains the possibility that the opening up of backward areas to settlement by the excess population of agricultural countries might be undertaken as an international matter. In other words, the task of developing a particular territory to the point where it could support migrants from European countries might be successfully undertaken by the joint action of a number of states, pooling their resources and sharing in the burden of administration. Such a scheme would afford to the native population greater safeguards against exploitation. It would likewise prevent the territory from being developed to the exclusive advantages of one state. There are of course difficulties associated with all proposals of internationalization of territory, but the possibility is at least worth careful exploration. This subject will be discussed in the last chapter.

CHAPTER FOUR

THE PROCEDURES OF PEACEFUL CHANGE

THE international procedures available for changes in rights or possessions are diplomatic negotiation, conciliation (including mediation), international conference and, indirectly, adjudication, which comprises both arbitration and judicial settlement. The conscious effort to change existing rules of law is called international legislation and is customarily effected through the procedure of the international conference, although it might also be brought about through diplomatic negotiation or even adjudication. These international procedures find concrete expression in the international institutions with which we are all familiar, namely, the diplomatic machinery, the League of Nations, commissions of inquiry, conciliation committees, arbitration tribunals, the Permanent Court of International Justice, *ad hoc* and periodic conferences.[1]

The most significant thing to note about these international procedures of peaceful change is that

[1] The method of the *fait accompli* is often included among the international procedures of peaceful change. However, since it is necessarily unilateral in character it is really not an international procedure, and hence will not be considered here. Furthermore, it has no juridical standing, whereas all the procedures mentioned above are recognized by international law. Finally, it does not become effective legally until recognized, and such recognition can only take place through one of the above procedures.

they are all, with but one very limited exception, *voluntary* with the nations concerned. Theoretically, if a nation, for whatever reason, is disinclined to approve of a change in the existing distribution of rights, the matter is ended. No provision is made for the coercion of the recalcitrant state. This is in accord with the legal concept that international law is based on the consent of nations and rights established thereunder cannot be changed except with the approval of every nation affected.

The one exception is the decision of an international tribunal which operates to change the law or the rights of the parties and which is rendered in pursuance of an agreement of compulsory adjudication. But this is of limited significance from the standpoint of peaceful change. It will be pointed out later that, while adjudication does result in extensive changes in law and in rights, the process is largely an unconscious and unintentional by-product, and nations consciously seeking changes in the status quo do not ordinarily resort to adjudication to achieve them. Hence it will be seen that in practically every instance of a demand for change in the status quo, the only international procedures available are, from a legal standpoint, voluntary and not obligatory procedures.

It is plain that this feature makes the problem of peaceful change exceedingly difficult. Of course if the nations concerned are willing or can readily be persuaded to make a particular change, the question of procedure offers no difficulty. They may follow whatever procedure they like. But that is not often the case. The typical situation involves a definite clash of interests in which one nation demands something that is in the lawful possession of another, and the latter clings tenaciously to it and refuses even to discuss the possibility of giving it up. This situation is exemplified in the attitude of the British Government toward the demands of Germany for the return of her colonies and in the attitude of the Little Entente toward the demands of Hungary for a revision of the territorial settlement of the Treaty of Trianon.

But there are many situations involving demands for peaceful change which are by no means beyond the range of peaceful solution. There are ways of inducing a nation to yield to a particular demand in the interest of peace and friendly relations. There are even ways of bringing pressure which are not incompatible with the notion of independence. Sometimes it is possible to devise means of compensation acceptable to the state asked to give up something it is entitled to under law. Occasionally an impartial inquiry by an outside agency will reveal a compromise that is satisfactory to both sides. In some instances when a state demands territory in order to satisfy certain needs it is found possible to meet the needs in some other manner than by territorial change. Not infrequently a strong state will yield up something desired by another state when it is realized that the price of opposing the change is a constantly increasing burden of armament, or when the other state persists in its demands with such tenacity that to yield is the lesser of two evils. While it is true that, in a society organized on the basis of "self-help", the advantage in a dispute is with the physically stronger nation, it is possible on occasion to organize pressures in such a manner that the differential in physical strength becomes less significant. Finally it may be possible sometimes to transfer a clash of interests from a bilateral competition into a question of general welfare, and thus to introduce considerations that definitely alter the relative power positions of the contending parties.

In brief, the problem of peaceful change calls for procedures adapted to persuasion, investigation, the discovery of compromises, the revealing of real interests and objectives, the determination of the general welfare, the organization of opposition, the marshalling of public opinion, the manipulation of pressures and means of coercion short of actual resort to hostilities. These are things with which the human race has been familiar for a very long time. They are capable of wide application in the settlement of demands for alterations in the status quo.

Diplomatic Negotiation

Diplomatic negotiation is of course the most readily available and the most frequently used procedure for discussing demands for change in the status quo. In this procedure the claim for redistribution will most likely be discussed in terms of the individual interests of the nations directly concerned, rather than in terms of any general community interest that might be involved. Presumably any solution arrived at by this method will have the agreement of all parties directly concerned. Actually, where there is disagreement in the beginning, this may be resolved either by barter or by pressure. Which of these two elements is dominant in a particular case will depend primarily on the power relationship of the parties. In a dispute between two Great Powers of approximately equal strength, the give and take of the bargaining process will be present in a greater degree than in a dispute between a Great Power and a small one. The "voluntary" character of the acquiescence by the small Power may be in the form of a choice between evils. This seems to be an inevitable accompaniment of the present stage of organization of the international community.

Many examples of peaceful change through diplomatic negotiation have been provided by the efforts of nations of restricted sovereignty to obtain their full freedom. Egypt in recent years offers a good illustration of how such changes may be accomplished.

Prior to 1922 Egypt had been a British protectorate. In 1922, in order to quiet nationalist unrest which amounted almost to an outright rebellion, Great Britain granted a limited form of independence. The Egyptians were permitted to have a constitutional monarchy with a cabinet responsible to an elected parliament. Great Britain, however, reserved the rights most essential to her imperial interests, notably the defense of the Suez Canal, the protection of Egypt against territorial aggression or interference by any Power, the preservation of foreign interests and property, and the administration of the Anglo-Egyptian Sudan.[2] The British military forces remained in Egypt and many British officials retained positions of authority in the Egyptian civil service.

The nationalists continued their agitation for the termination of British control and of capitulations without notable success. However, the situation was altered in 1935 by Italy's conquest of Ethiopia and sabre-rattling in Libya. On the one hand, the Egyptians were made more tractible by the realization that a certain amount of British protection was necessary if they were to avoid conquest by Italy or some other power. They also had come to realize

[2]*Egypt No. 1* (1922), Cmd. 1592.

that only with British aid could Egypt be rid of capitulations. On the other hand, Great Britain was faced with the possibility of having to fight Italy on the Libyan front, as well as elsewhere, and was accordingly in a mood to make terms with Egypt.

A new treaty was signed in London on August 27, 1936, and ratified December 23, 1936. By its terms, Great Britain promised to collaborate in using "every influence with the Powers exercising capitulary rights in Egypt" to bring about the termination of these rights.[3] Great Britain also recognized Egypt's independence to the extent of promising to support her entry into the League of Nations, to terminate British military occupation of Egypt, to allow Egypt entire responsibility for the protection of foreigners, to bring about the withdrawal of Englishmen from important positions in the Egyptian civil service, and to recognize Egypt's right to share in the administration of the Sudan. At the same time, Egypt remained within British protection so far as her external relations were concerned. Great Britain was authorized to station forces in the vicinity of the Canal "with a view to insuring in coöperation with the Egyptian forces the defense of the Canal," and this was to continue "until such time as the parties agree that the

[3]The twelve capitulary Powers on May 8, 1937, at Montreux signed a convention providing for the abolition of the capitulations. (*New York Times*, May 9, 1937, I, 22.)

Egyptian army is strong enough to insure by its own resources the liberty and entire security of navigation of the Canal."[4] British military advisers were to help to develop a small Egyptian army and air force.

This is an example of peaceful change sought by a small Power which was at first opposed by a Great Power but which was subsequently achieved in substantial measure through the procedure of diplomatic negotiation. It is true that the changed attitude of Great Britain was due in large part to the Italian invasion of Ethiopia, but it was also due to the development of strong leadership in Egypt and to the ability of the various factions finally to forget their differences and present a united front to Great Britain.[5]

There have been numerous other examples of peaceful change of the status quo brought about through the procedure of diplomatic negotiation. The United States has on various occassions acquired territory in this manner. Thus in 1917 it acquired the Virgin Islands from Denmark by purchase. It is true that the "voluntary" character of the sale is not very convincing in view of Secretary of State Lansing's advice to the Danish Minister in Washington that

[4]Pierre Crabitès, "Egypt Signs a Treaty," *Current History,* January, 1937.

[5]*Ibid.*

in the event of an evident intention on the part of Germany to take possession of his country or to compel Denmark to cede the islands to her, the United States would be under the necessity of seizing and annexing them, and, though it would be done with the greatest reluctance, it would be necessary to do it in order to avoid a serious dispute with the German Government over the sovereignty of and title to the islands, as we would never permit the group to become German.[6]

However, since the transfer was effected without the direct resort to force or the *fait accompli,* it falls within the definition of peaceful change. Among the other instances in which the United States has acquired territory through diplomatic negotiation are the purchase of Alaska from Russia in 1867, the "Gadsden Purchase" from Mexico in 1853, and the Louisiana Purchase in 1803.

In 1890 the United Kingdom ceded Heligoland to Germany as a counterpoise in the partition of Africa. In 1899 Great Britain withdrew from the Anglo-German-American condominium in Samoa, receiving in compensation part of the German Solomon Islands and leaving Germany and the United States to divide the Samoan Islands between them.

In 1924 the Soviet-Japanese Treaty secured the evacuation by Japan of Northern Sakhalin, held since 1918, and its full restoration to the Soviet Government in return for which Japan received oil

[6]Robert Lansing, "Drama of the Virgin Islands Purchase," *New York Times Magazine,* July 19, 1931, p. 4.

and coal concessions. In 1911 France ceded 100,000 square miles of the French Congo to Germany in return for recognition by Germany of the French protectorate over Morocco following the Agadir incident. By the Treaty of Carlstad of September 23, 1906, the Swedish Government accepted the decree of the Norwegian *Storthing* dethroning the Swedish King and declaring Norwegian independence from Sweden, the decree having been endorsed by a plebiscite of the Norwegian people.

As an example of a change in the status quo not involving a transfer of territorial sovereignty may be cited the Treaty between the United States and Cuba in 1934 abolishing the Platt Amendment. Another example is the Hay-Pauncefote Treaty of 1901 in which Great Britain renounced her claim under the Clayton-Bulwer Treaty to an equal voice with the United States in the control of the Isthmian Canal.

Conciliation

Conciliation is a procedure which has often been used in connection with disputes as to legal rights but seldom in connection with claims for changes in the status quo. This procedure (which includes mediation) is similar to diplomatic negotiation save that a third party is present. The third party may be another nation or it may be an agency like the League of Nations, which is empowered to exercise conciliation functions under Articles 11 and 15 of the Covenant. While the mediating agency is presumably interested only in aiding the disputing Powers to find a solution acceptable to both sides, its presence undoubtedly alters the power relationship of the parties and hence the nature of the procedure of agreement. Here also it is presumed that any solution arrived at is acceptable to the parties concerned. However, if the disputing nations are weak, the action of the mediator may in fact represent pressure.

An outstanding example of peaceful change by conciliation is the Shantung settlement arrived at in 1922, which involved the restoration to China of Japanese rights and holdings, including transfer of the leased territory of Kiaochao and sale of the Tsingtao-Tsinanfu Railway to China, and also the rendition to China of the British leased territory of Weihaiwei.

Although Japan's possession of former German rights in the Shantung Peninsula was recognized by the Treaty of Versailles, her position there and elsewhere had aroused considerable anti-Japanese feeling not only in China but also in Russia, the United States, Canada and Australia. China had refused to sign the Treaty of Versailles, and a Chinese boycott of Japanese goods had proved highly effective. In the United States there were numerous expressions of strong opposition, both official and private, to the continuation of Japanese control in Shantung, and force was given to this opposition by the plans of the United States for constructing a navy far beyond anything possible to Japanese resources. At the same time the Anglo-Japanese Alliance was about to be terminated in response to Canadian and Australian demands.

Thus it was clear to Japan at the time of the Washington Conference that her position in Shantung would have to be liquidated. She had hoped to do this through private conversations with China in either Tokyo or Peking, where she would enjoy the full advantage of being the stronger Power. On the other hand, China wanted the matter put on the agenda of the Washington Conference, objecting to direct conversations, first, because they would be prejudicial to her as the weaker state, and second, because her consent to negotiations would imply that Japan possessed negotiable rights in Shantung.

The actual procedure was a compromise worked out by the British and American delegates to the Washington Conference. It consisted of conversations technically private in accordance with the wish of the Japanese Government. But while they were carried on outside the Conference proper, they were definitely collateral to it, their results being announced to the Conference and forming an integral part of its general Far Eastern settlement. The conversations were thus carried on in an atmosphere favorable to China and were conducted in pursuance of the good offices of Hughes and Balfour in the presence of their representatives who made suggestions. They were, furthermore, based entirely on the *de facto* situation irrespective of legal or treaty rights.[7]

This procedure resulted in a bipartite treaty which restored the leased territory of Kiaochao, provided for the withdrawal of Japanese troops from the Tsingtao-Tsinanfu Railway and from Tsingtao, and transferred the Tsingtao-Tsinanfu Railway to China. Mines in which rights had been granted to Germany were to be handed over to a company under Chinese charter in which Japanese capital could not exceed Chinese.[8] Two joint commissions of three members from each country arranged the details on the spot. Japan's *quid pro quo* for the restoration of Shantung and other concessions was naval security in the Western Pacific, resulting from acceptance by the United States of naval limitation and agreement to maintain the status quo in regard to naval bases and fortifications in the Pacific islands.

As a make-weight in arranging the restoration of Japanese holdings in Shantung, Great Britain gave up her lease of the territory of Weihaiwei in Shan-

[7]Westal W. Willoughby, *China at the Conference: A Report* (Baltimore, 1922), Chap. XXIII.

[8]"Treaty for the Settlement of Outstanding Questions Relative to Shantung," *Ibid.*, p. 391, ff.

tung, which she had held since 1898. After the announcement of the Chinese-Japanese Agreement at the Fifth Plenary Session of the Washington Conference on February 1, 1922, Balfour stated that Great Britain would surrender her lease of Weihaiwei subject to availability of the territory as a sanitorium or summer resort for the China Squadron of the British Navy. This was accepted and confirmed by letter by the Chinese delegation. A Joint Commission began discussions on October 2, 1922, reaching a provisional agreement on May 31, 1923.[9] However, a final treaty was not signed until April 18, 1930. Ratifications and rendition took place on October 1, 1930.[10]

In form, the sale of Soviet interests in the Chinese Eastern Railway to Manchukuo in 1934-35 was conducted by a procedure of conciliation. The Soviet Government had originally proposed to sell its interests to Japan, but the latter insisted that the sale must be made to Manchukuo, Japan acting only as an intermediary. The U. S. S. R. gave way on this point and Japan thereby gained indirect recognition of Manchukuo. The negotiations took place in Tokyo between the Soviet Government and Manchukuo, with the mediation of Japan. Actually the relationship between the purchaser, Manchukuo, and the mediator, Japan, is such that it is very diffi-

[9]British Institute of International Affairs, *Survey of International Affairs*, 1920-1923, p. 463; Willoughby, *op. cit.*, pp. 189-191.

[10]*Survey of International Affairs*, 1930, pp. 351-2.

cult to regard this as a genuine example of peaceful change by the procedure of conciliation.

An example of this procedure in which an international organization acted as mediator is found in the dispute concerning the cancellation by the Persian Government of the concession of the Anglo-Persian Oil Company. This dispute was submitted to the Council of the League of Nations by Great Britain in 1932. Following mediation by the Council's *rapporteur,* M. Benes, a new concession more favorable to the Persian Government was agreed upon by the Company and the Persian Government.

International Conferences

International conferences may be divided roughly, from a procedural standpoint, into two types, bargaining conferences and legislative conferences.[11] The first type is concerned primarily with resolving conflicts of interest or rights among a group of states by contractual arrangement. The second type is concerned with laying down rules of conduct for the group as a whole. This second type is the principal agency of international legislation and will be considered under that heading. Only the first type will be dealt with here, that is, the con-

[11]Reference is here made only to conferences held in time of peace. Conferences held at the conclusion of wars are excluded because the changes they effect, being the direct result of a resort to force, cannot be regarded as examples of peaceful change.

ference concerned chiefly with altering the existing distribution of rights or possessions of the participating states.

In international conferences of this type the situation is much the same as in conciliation, except that the third party being a group of states instead of a single mediator a multiplicity of interests and pressures is introduced. Here again presumably no solution is arrived at except by the voluntary agreement of the parties concerned. However, the manner in which the interests and powers are distributed among the participating states will have a profound influence on the outcome. Thus if enough of the larger Powers are in agreement on a particular solution there will be overwhelming force behind it and pressure can be applied to compel acceptance of the recommended change. The action is still regarded as voluntary and the change as peaceful. On the other hand, if the larger Powers are not in agreement there is no overwhelming force and pressure cannot be applied in favor of a particular solution. If the parties remain in disagreement the nation demanding the change may resort to war to obtain it. The first case, in which the superior force of the larger Powers is the important element in bringing about a particular change, is nevertheless a case of peaceful change because force is not actually used. The second case, in which the strength of the larger Powers is not brought to bear and the parties are left free to choose their own course of action, becomes in the end a case of forceful change.

An admirable example of altering the status quo through the conference method is the settlement arrived at by the Congress of Berlin in 1878. This conference represents in the minds of many people an unpalatable illustration of power politics. At the same time it is an undeniable case of peaceful change, because it facilitated the redistribution of certain territories in the Near East and thus prevented a war which would undoubtedly have broken out to realize the same end. It likewise illustrates how, in an agreement of the bargaining type, the relative power positions of the parties are reflected in the terms of the agreement, although the acceptance of the agreement is presumably entirely voluntary on the part of the signatories.

As is well known, the Congress of Berlin prevented a war between Great Britain and Austria on the one side and Russia on the other by re-establishing the balance of power in the Near East which Russia had attempted to tip in her favor in the Treaty of San Stefano. In order to accomplish this end the Congress not only revised the Treaty of San Stefano but also revised portions of the map of the Near East untouched by the Treaty of San Stefano.

Both Great Britain and Austria were determined to prevent Russian supremacy in the Near East, which threatened to result from the Russo-Turkish War of 1877-78. Moreover, the Treaty of San Stefano which terminated that war contained provisions in direct conflict with secret agreements made by Austria and Russia in 1876 and 1877. In those agreements Russia had promised that in case of territorial changes in the Turkish Empire, Austria would be permitted to occupy Bosnia and Herzegovina. Furthermore, there was to be no great Slav state in the Near East.[12] But the Treaty of San Stefano created an extensive Bulgaria and did not deliver Bosnia and Herzegovina to Austria. By that treaty Russia was to receive part of Armenia, a strip of the Dobrudja (which she planned to trade with Rumania for Bessarabia), and a war indemnity so large that Turkey would need a long time to repay it, thus giving Russia a continuous excuse for interfering in Turkish affairs. Various other territorial changes were provided for by the treaty.[13]

It became clear that Russia was faced with the choice of submitting her gains to a conference of the Powers or going to war with Great Britain and Austria. She finally gave way and agreed to a congress in Berlin to consider all clauses of the Treaty. The formal invitations to the Congress were issued

[12]Conference between Austria and Russia at Reichstadt, July, 1876, and the Conventions of January and April, 1877. See E. L. Woodward, *The Congress of Berlin, 1878* (London, 1919), pp. 3-4.

[13]*State Papers,* Vol. 69, p. 732.

by the German Government on June 3 and the Congress met from June 13 to July 13, 1878.

The success of the Congress in reaching agreement had been assured by a series of more or less secret bilateral agreements between the interested parties.[14] These agreements provided the outlines for the Treaty of Berlin, signed on July 13, 1878, which formed a compromise among the conflicting desires of Austria and Russia and England at the expense of the Turkish Empire. By this Treaty Russia was allowed to retain the Armenian territory gained under the Treaty of San Stefano, and she also secured the retrocession of the Rumanian strip of Bessarabia, Rumania being poorly compensated with the Dobrudja. Austria's share was the right to occupy Bosnia-Herzegovina and to keep garrisons and maintain roads in the Sanjak of Novibazar. Bulgaria was split into three parts and the independence of Rumania, Serbia and Montenegro was recognized, while Greece gained Thessaly.[15] The British compensation was found, not in the Treaty of Berlin, but in the Anglo-Turkish Convention of June 4, 1878, according to which Great Britain guaranteed Turkey against further Russian aggrandizement in Asia Minor, the Sultan promised far-reaching reforms in the government of his Christian subjects, and as a pledge of the latter Great Britain was

[14]Cf. Henry F. Munro, *The Berlin Congress* (Washington, 1918), p. 5.

[15]*State Papers*, 69, p. 749; Cf. Woodward, *op. cit.*, pp. 32-35.

to be allowed to hold and administer Cyprus.[16] While this convention was bilateral, it was acquiesced in by the Powers at the Congress.

France received nothing directly from the Congress of Berlin but was secretly urged by England and Germany to compensate herself in Tunis.[17] Germany acted as mediator both before and during the Congress. She made no claims and Bismarck asserted that his rôle was merely that of an "honest broker." He was in fact uninterested in the Near East so far as Germany was concerned. However, he used his influence to support Austria's eastern ambitions, which he believed would strengthen her acceptance of the German Empire under Prussian hegemony.

There have been many other instances of peaceful changes of rights or possessions effected or confirmed by international conferences. Thus in 1864 the United Kingdom announced to the signatories of the Treaty of 1815 her willingness to renounce her protectorate over the Ionian Islands and recognize their union with Greece, and a conference of the signatories accepted this revision. In 1867 a conference of the Powers at London neutralized and demilitarized the Grand Duchy of Luxembourg under international guarantee, the King of the Netherlands retaining the sovereignty and the Prussian

[16]*State Papers,* 69, p. 744, ff.; Woodward, *op. cit.,* pp. 17-19.

[17]Woodward, p. 42; Parker T. Moon, *Imperialism and World Politics* (New York, 1926), p. 238.

garrison being withdrawn. In 1870 Russia, with Germany's support, denounced the portion of the Treaty of Paris of 1856 which limited Russian naval forces and armaments in the Black Sea, and a conference of the Powers in London in 1871 ratified the act.

The Berlin Conference of 1884-85 was both a bargaining and a legislative conference; it recognized the existence of the Congo Free State and agreed on the general principles for trade and colonial enterprise in equatorial Africa. In 1923 Tangier was internationalized by the Statute of Tangier, drawn up by a conference attended by Great Britain, France and Spain and later revised and adhered to by all of the signatories of the Act of Algerciras except the United States (Germany's rights having passed to France). The Lausanne Conference of 1932 abolished the reparation clauses of the Treaty of Versailles and provided for later payment by Germany of 3,000,000 gold marks into a European reconstruction fund in place of reparations. In 1936 the provisions of the Treaty of Lausanne of 1923 pertaining to the internationalization of the Straits were revised by a conference of the signatories (exclusive of Italy which, however, subsequently accepted the revision[18]), the revised treaty permitting the remilitarization of the Straits by Turkey. On May 8, 1937, a conference of capitulary Powers

[18] *New York Times,* January 3, 1937, p. 30.

signed a convention providing for the termination of capitulations in Egypt.

International Legislation

In the normal political community the customary procedure for bringing about changes in the status quo which are beyond the range of voluntary contractual agreement of the parties is legislation. Under this procedure claims for alteration in rights or in law are presumably considered in the light of the general interest of the community, and this general interest necessarily overrides any conflicting individual interest. Since there are almost always present one or more conflicting individual interests, the determination of the general interest must be arrived at by something less than the unanimous action of all members of the community. In a democracy this may be by some form of majority vote; in an autocracy by a small minority or even by a single individual. In any event some enforcing machinery is necessary to make the dominant will prevail over the conflicting group or groups. In the ideal state, perhaps, the individual members would have such a lively appreciation of the general welfare that they would voluntarily and freely forego any interest of their own which seemed to conflict. But in the everyday world, such enlightenment is not often encountered. The important questions regarding legislation are, first, what part of the community shall determine the community interest, and, second, how shall the decision be enforced.

Attempts have been made to develop effective legislative machinery in the international community, but so far without notable success. So long as "self-help" remains the ultimate basis of international relations, governments will be very slow about yielding up to a central legislative organ any authority to change the status quo in such manner as to affect in the slightest degree their power, their ability to defend themselves or to make their will prevail in dealings with other nations. So important do nations regard the capacity to maintain their independence that they will not even permit an outside agency to decide whether a particular condition is or is not necessary to their national defense. The result of this is that nations cannot be induced to join in the establishment of any legislative machinery with the power to override them on any specific issue which might have any bearing on their power or independence. In other words, any international legislative machinery with authority to touch existing rights or possessions can only operate on the basis of unanimous action and will not be permitted to make the general welfare prevail over the conflicting interests of any single nation.

So long as this condition exists it will limit very sharply the possible scope of international legislation in the political relations of nations. There has been a very large amount of conscious law making in the international field in recent years, but it has been confined almost entirely to the so-called non-political field, *i.e.,* to matters which are not regarded as directly affecting the existence, independence or status of a nation. Thus a notable body of legislation has been achieved in the fields of communication and transit, health, and public welfare, labor, and economic and financial relations.[19] In these fields it has been possible to develop a consciousness of common interests and to achieve unanimity of agreement, largely because the question of the security of states is not involved.

International legislation is, of course, normally the product of a multipartite conference, either an *ad hoc* conference or one of the periodic or special conferences of an international organization, such as, for example, the International Labor Organization or the Communications and Transit Organization.

It is true that even on political matters nations reach unanimous agreement surprisingly often. Here again there are ways of inducing recalcitrant states not to stand out against the general welfare, and the techniques for bringing about unanimous consent are constantly improving.[20] But genuine leg-

[19]See the four large volumes of *International Legislation,* edited by Manley O. Hudson, covering only the period between 1919 and 1929 (Washington, 1931).

[20]For an account of the various ways that have been developed to lessen the rigors of the unanimity requirement in the Covenant of the League of Nations, see Cromwell A. Riches, *The Unanimity Rule and the League of Nations* (Baltimore, 1933), Chapters III-V.

islative machinery will not be achieved in the international field until it is possible to get away from the unanimity rule in matters regarded as political. This is not likely to happen until self-help ceases to be the ultimate basis of international existence and independence.

A recent example of peaceful change through international legislation was the termination of Iraq's mandatory status by her admission to the League of Nations by unanimous vote of the Assembly on October 3, 1932.[21] The mandatory power, Great Britain, did not oppose the change, and in fact had been working toward it since 1920. There had been a gradual transfer of executive responsibility to Iraq officials and the number of British officials had been decreased from nearly 3,000 in 1920 to 196 in 1931.[22] In fact Great Britain seems to have been in a greater hurry to get out in the end than the Permanent Mandates Commission was to have her leave, the latter being concerned about the plight of non-Arab minorities in Iraq.[23]

[21]The Council had previously agreed that termination of the mandatory régime would be "effective only as from the date on which Iraq has been admitted to the League of Nations." (*Official Journal of the League of Nations,* 1932, p. 474.)

[22]*Survey of International Affairs,* 1934, p. 179.

[23]Note, for example, the statement in the Commission's special report of November, 1931, that "the Commission would, for its part, have been unable to contemplate the termination of a régime which appeared some years ago to be necessary in the interests of all sections of the Population," had it not been for the declaration of the Mandatory Power at the Twentieth Session of the Mandates Commission that moral responsibility, "should Iraq prove herself unworthy of the confidence which had been placed in her," must

It is true that Iraq's strategic value to Great Britain is immense. It lies along the shortest route from Great Britain to India and promises to be the aerial Suez Canal. However, the burden of carrying the mandate was very great, especially in view of the growing Iraq nationalism, and Great Britain's strategic position could be maintained practically as well by a strong alliance. A treaty of alliance, ratified in 1931, was part of the bargain, leaving Great Britain the paramount Power so far as Iraq's foreign relations were concerned. This treaty provided for, first, consultation in all matters of foreign policy affecting the common interests of the two Powers; second, an agreement to come to each other's assistance in the event of war; third, permission to Great Britain to maintain military forces and two air bases for British squadrons in Iraq; and fourth, collaboration in Iraq's defense.[24]

Article 19 of the League Covenant and the Revision of Treaties

It is often said that the problem of peaceful change is a problem of treaty revision, and that the way to solve it is to improve the machinery for altering treaty provisions that have become out of date. To this end special attention is given to the possi-

rest with the British Government. (*Minutes of the Permanent Mandates Commission,* Twentieth Session, p. 134, Twenty-First Session, Annex 22.)

[24]*League of Nations Treaty Series,* Vol. 132, No. 3048.

bility of improving the procedure specified in Article 19 of the Covenant of the League of Nations.

It is true that most of the situations which nations desire to change are embodied in treaties, and it is not possible to change the situations without revising the treaties. But it is also true that the treaty provision is merely the written expression of an agreement already reached by one or more of the procedures mentioned above. The treaty does not come into existence until there has taken place the striking of a bargain or the balancing of forces or pressures or whatever it is that leads to an agreement in the first place. In like manner, changing the situation incorporated in a treaty can only come about through the procedures available for reaching an agreement. Once this has been done, the revision of the treaty is a comparatively simple matter. But it is a delusion to suppose that improving techniques for the formal revision of treaties is going to remove the difficulties of arriving at an agreement in the first place. No machinery of revision, for example, can disguise the fact that the international procedures available for reaching agreement are primarily procedures of persuasion, and that such procedures are definitely limited in the face of established attitudes and conceptions of vital interests.

To say that the problem of peaceful change is a problem of treaty revision is like saying that the problem of the relations between capital and labor is one of revision of contracts. It is true that the bargains struck between employer and employee are usually put in contract form, but it is idle to suppose that the constant clash of interests between the two groups is due to any lack of procedures for altering contracts.

There seems to be considerable disappointment over the fact that Article 19 of the League Covenant has not served as a more useful instrument of peaceful change. Perhaps a good deal of this feeling is due to a failure to distinguish between the procedure of arriving at an agreement and the formalities of putting that agreement into effect. The text of Article 19 is as follows:

> The Assembly may from time to time advise the reconsideration by Members of the League of treaties which have become inapplicable and the consideration of international conditions whose continuance might endanger the peace of the world.

The original purpose of this article was apparently not to provide a general procedure for revising treaties but rather a means for making territorial adjustments as part of the collective system of territorial guaranty contained in Article 10. In President Wilson's first draft the substance of Article 19 formed a part of Article 3 which later became Article 10. This draft was as follows:[25]

[25]David Hunter Miller, *The Drafting of the Covenant,* Vol. 2, p. 12.

The contracting powers unite in guaranteeing to each other political independence and territorial integrity; but it is understood between them that such territorial readjustments, if any, as may in the future become necessary by reason of changes in present racial conditions and aspirations or present social and political relationships, pursuant to the principle of self-determination, and also such territorial readjustments as may in the judgment of three-fourths of the delegates (at the Assembly) be demanded by the welfare and manifest interest of the peoples concerned, may be effected, if agreeable to those peoples; and that territorial changes may in equity involve material compensation. The contracting powers accept without reservation the principle that the peace of the world is superior in importance to every question of political jurisdictional boundary.

President Wilson realized that there were bound to be mistakes and inequities in the territorial settlement agreed upon at the close of the War, and that if this settlement was to be guaranteed there would have to be some means of making adjustments in it. He believed that later on, when war passions had cooled, the nations would be in a better frame of mind to make such adjustments. He saw likewise that if such adjustments were to be made through the League of Nations, the unanimity rule would have to be modified for this purpose. But the subject of territorial revision is the one which touches most closely upon the security and independence of nations, and they look with extreme suspicion upon any move to endow an international agency with the authority even to discuss such matters.

In its final form Article 19 became an innocuous invitation to hear complaints about the territorial settlement and "advise" as to possible revisions, but no procedure was specified for carrying out this function, nor was any authority given to override opposition. Clearly the Assembly cannot by its own act alter the provisions of any treaty or transfer any territory. Apparently the most that the Article contemplates is that the Assembly might cause an investigation to be made and that as a result thereof it would make recommendations which would have a persuasive effect on the nations directly concerned. But it is by no means clear that Article 19 is not covered by Article 5, which requires that, unless otherwise expressly provided, decisions of the Assembly must be unanimous.[26] This requirement would prevent the Assembly even from advising in any case in which there was opposition. But if there was no opposition, no action by the Assembly would be necessary. If it should be argued that the unanimity requirement does not include the parties concerned in the matter, one can only recall that the

[26]The writers are at odds on this point. Thus Professor Quincy Wright holds that a unanimous vote is required, including the nations directly concerned in the dispute. Professor Tobin seems to favor the view that only a majority is required, with the parties to the treaty participating. Professor Riches holds that only a majority is required, with the parties to the Treaty excluded. See Quincy Wright, "Article 19 of the League Covenant and the Doctrine 'Rebus Sic Stantibus'." *Proceedings, American Society of International Law,* April 23-25, 1936, p. 70; Harold J. Tobin, *The Termination of Multipartite Treaties* (New York, 1933), p. 290; Cromwell A. Riches, *op. cit.,* pp. 155-157.

majority of territorial settlements are made in multilateral treaties to which a large number of states are parties. If all the signatories had to be excluded in such a case, the recommendation of the Assembly would not be very persuasive. If it should finally be established that only a majority is required, the persuasive value of an Assembly resolution would still be slight in any case in which a state felt that its vital interests were involved.

Article 19 has been a dead letter from the beginning, and it would seem useless to try to implement it while retaining its present general form. If the League is to be given any effective power to aid in the revision of treaties, Article 19 would have to be replaced by a provision making decisions binding on the parties, with adequate means of enforcement. The unanimity rule would likewise have to be modified.[27]

Commissions of Inquiry

The proposal most frequently heard for improving Article 19 is to make provision for the appointment of Commissions of Inquiry to investigate the facts on which claims for treaty revision are based and report upon the merits thereof. The theory is

[27]Cf. the suggestion along this line contained in the memorandum by le Fur and de la Pradelle on "The Revision of Treaties," printed in *Collective Security*, Maurice Bourquin, ed., (Paris, 1936), pp. 195-201. A number of other discussions of Article XIX will be found in Chapter III of the same work.

that an unbiased statement of the facts might indicate a solution that would be satisfactory to both sides, and that at least it would influence public opinion, which would in turn operate to induce the nations concerned to arrive at a peaceful settlement.

The idea of the Commission of Inquiry is of course an old one, and many efforts have been made to develop it into an effective procedure for the pacific settlement of international disputes. A number of treaties have in fact been concluded in recent years providing for the establishment of such commissions for the investigation of the facts of future disputes between the signatories.[28] It is commonly believed that nations involved in disputes will be less apt to object to the establishment of Commissions of Inquiry than to any other procedure, since the findings of such Commissions are in no way binding on anyone.

It seems to be true that the Commission of Inquiry method is more useful in some types of demands than in others. It undoubtedly has considerable utility in connection with claims based on legal right, since the determination of the legal rights of the parties often turns upon the determination of a particular set of facts pertinent to the legal issue involved. But in the case of changes in the status quo, the utility of the method, taken by itself, is not

[28]Cf. Max Habicht, *Post-War Treaties for the Pacific Settlement of International Disputes* (Cambridge, 1931), p. 1001 ff.

so clear. The chief difficulty is to know what facts the Commission is to be empowered to collect. In questions of peaceful change, especially those involving territorial revision, considerations of national power and prestige are usually present and often paramount. Are these the types of facts which the disinterested Commission of Inquiry is supposed to investigate? Nations are not in practice willing to have facts of this character determined by any one but themselves. Furthermore, nations make demands of this character on the basis of felt needs or desires, in other words, on value judgments, and such judgments are usually not altered by simple factual investigation. It is of course true that disinterested factual investigation is always useful in passing upon claims of any character, but it does not seem to offer, by itself, an effective method of disposing of claims for peaceful change.[29]

[29]While the Lytton Commission acted in connection with a situation in which a resort to force had already occurred rather than one in which a mere threat of force existed, it is interesting in the present connection, both because it represents the most ambitious attempt, to date, at an impartial finding of fact and because it proposed a solution involving change in the legal situation. Its terms of reference required it both to find facts and to "contribute towards a final and fundamental solution of the questions at issue." In the final chapters of its report it proposed certain alterations in the situation existing prior to September, 1931, including autonomy for Manchuria within China. While China acquiesced in the proposals and the Assembly of the League of Nations accepted the Lytton Commission's proposals as a basis of settlement, Japan, of course, refused. In other words, the facts as the Commission found them did not make clear a solution which would at once be compatible with the interests of China and the other Powers having interests there, and the desires of Japan.

International Adjudication

The procedure of international adjudication comprises both arbitration and judicial settlement. It envisages the hearing of claims by an impartial tribunal which decides them in accordance with law, the decision being binding on the parties.

The common notion that international arbitration tribunals are not really courts of law, and that they are free to find compromises satisfactory to the parties, is erroneous. They are as much judicial bodies as any other courts, and are bound to reach their decisions in accordance with the law. They cannot be half judicial and half non-judicial at the same time. The difference between arbitration and judicial settlement is not in the procedure followed in reaching a decision but in the temporary or permanent nature of the tribunal. Arbitration tribunals are *ad hoc* bodies created to decide specific disputes after these disputes have arisen and going out of existence when the dispute is decided. Judicial settlement refers to the action of permanent courts already in existence before a particular dispute arises. Both bodies decide in accordance with the law and cannot depart from it unless specifically authorized by the terms of reference.

Since adjudication means deciding in accordance with the law, it obviously is not a procedure that is specially adapted to changing the law. Where the law on a particular question is well settled and clear, a nation desiring to change that law or its rights thereunder would not be apt to resort to arbitration or judicial settlement to do so. However strong its reasons for desiring a change, the tribunal could but affirm the existing law. Thus Germany does not resort to adjudication to settle her claim for the return of her colonies because she knows what the answer would be. Any court of law would have to recognize the sovereignty of the existing holders, regardless of Germany's economic necessities.

However, it would be quite erroneous to suppose that adjudication does not result in changes in the status quo. As a matter of fact it is constantly effecting changes both in rights and in rules of law. But the process is often unconscious and unintentional and is done under the guise of finding the existing law.

On rare occasions an international tribunal will actually be given the power to decide upon new rules of law which will be binding upon the parties. A notable example of this was the Behring Sea Arbitration between the United States and Great Britain. The main question at issue in that case was whether the United States had exclusive jurisdiction of the Behring Sea and could seize British fishing vessels for improper or wasteful methods of sealing. The treaty of arbitration provided that if the Arbitration Commission found that the United

States did not have exclusive jurisdiction of the Behring Sea, it should then decide upon regulations for the preservation of the seals. This action of the Commission was to be binding on the parties. The Commission did find against the United States and did draw up a set of regulations which were duly put into effect.[30]

The North Atlantic Fisheries Arbitration might also be regarded as an example of the direct granting of power to a tribunal to legislate for the parties, save that in this case the tribunal was only empowered to "recommend for the consideration of the High Contracting Parties rules and a method of procedure under which all questions which may arise in the future regarding the exercise of the liberties above referred to may be determined in accordance with the principles laid down in the award." It was further provided that if the parties did not adopt the rules and method of procedure recommended by the tribunal, then any future difference between the parties relating to the interpretation of the Treaty of 1818 or the effect and application of the award of the Tribunal should be referred informally to the Permanent Court of Arbitration at the Hague for decision by the summary procedure provided for in the Hague Convention of 1907.[31] The rules and

[30]Cf. John Bassett Moore, *A Digest of International Law* (Washington, 1906), I, 890-923.

[31]W. M. Malloy, *Treaties, Conventions,* etc. (Washington, 1910), Vol. I, p. 835 ff.

procedures recommended by the Tribunal were in fact accepted by the two nations and duly put into effect.[32]

In a sense, every specific application of law to a particular set of facts is an act of legislation *in concreto*. For every case has some features that are peculiar to it, if only the names and identities of the parties. But for many cases there is no doubt about which rule of law applies, for example, cases which have arisen repeatedly in the past. In such cases it is of no significance to say that the Tribunal in applying the rule is engaging in legislation.

But where the novel feature of the case is of sufficient importance to cause doubt about which rule of law applies, then it might well be argued that the act of adjudication represents in fact legislation. In novel cases (which include practically all cases that go to litigation) the difficulty is not that there is no existing law to apply but that there is too much. Owing to the ambiguity of language and the breadth of meaning of legal terms it is normally possible to place a new case under two or more rules or principles of law, each leading to a different answer. That is precisely what the opposing sides in the case do, and it is then left to the tribunal to select between these competing rules or principles. The way in which judges make this selec-

[32] *Treaties, Conventions,* etc. (Washington, 1923). Vol. III, p. 2632 ff.

tion is an extremely complex subject and will not be gone into here. It may be said, however, that the result of the process is new law for the situation in question. For until the tribunal makes its selection, there is no way of knowing which rule or principle the set of facts will eventually find itself under. But this type of law-making is largely unconscious and, from the standpoint of the parties to the issue, unpredictable. It is clearly not a very useful procedure of peaceful change.

In the Behring Sea controversy mentioned above, the United States had claimed the right to restrain British subjects from killing seals in the Behring Sea in a manner which threatened to destroy the sealing industry. This was plainly a novel case in its important aspects, yet there were various legal principles lying about which, so far as the meaning of words was concerned, could easily be said to cover the situation. These principles led to different answers. The Arbitration Tribunal selected the principle of the freedom of the seas, which was clearly broad enough in its terms to include the case at issue if that seemed the appropriate way of disposing of the situation. Yet the Tribunal would have done no violence to law or logic had it selected instead the principle of "abuse of rights" and admitted that there was a right of protection of the seals. Professor Lauterpacht seems to think that the latter selection would have been more appropriate.[33]

In any case, the decision of the Tribunal may be regarded as legislation because until it was made there was no way of knowing for certain which of the several possible principles would be applied.

On occasion it is evident to everyone that a set of facts comes under a particular rule of law, but the results are, for one reason or another, unsatisfactory. It is usually possible, under all legal systems, for the court, without having any special authority, to avoid the unsatisfactory result by recourse to "higher law" or to "fundamental jurisprudence"; for example, to find that following the rule in the particular case would be contrary to the major purposes of the law as a whole. This again is a case of of judicial law-making under the guise of interpretation, but it is still not a satisfactory method for dealing with claims for peaceful change.

A notable example of this kind of judicial law-making is found in the opinion of the Permanent Court of International Justice in the case concerning the boundary between Iraq and Turkey. The question at issue was whether, in reaching a decision under Article 15 of the Covenant of the League of Nations, the votes of all members of the Council, including the parties to the dispute, had to be

[33]H. Lauterpacht, *The Function of Law in the International Community* (London, 1933), p. 98.

counted. Article 5 of the Covenant stipulates that, except where otherwise expressly provided, "decisions at any meeting of the Assembly or of the Council shall require the agreement of all the Members of the League represented at the meeting." To the average person the wording of this article seems quite clear and unambiguous. Yet the Court was able to find that this provision was subject to the "well-known rule that no one can be judge in his own suit," and hence the votes of the parties to the dispute should not be counted.[34] The good sense of this decision, from the standpoint of the practical working of the League, is obvious. Yet had the Court wanted to hold exactly the opposite, few would deny that Article 5 would have provided ample justification.

In this connection it is interesting to compare the decisions of two different arbitration tribunals rendered at approximately the same time on an identical question yet reaching opposite conclusions. The question at issue was whether, under international law, claims based on legal rights could be extinguished by lapse of time. In the *George W. Cook* case before the Mexican-American General Claims Commission, Mexico sought to have a claim ruled out on the ground of lapse of time, but the Commission found (June 3, 1927) that no rule of prescription

[34]*Permanent Court of International Justice,* Series B. No. 12, p. 32.

existed in international law and permitted the claim to be heard.[35] In the case of *Sarropoulos* v. *Bulgarian State,* decided by the Graeco-Bulgarian Mixed Arbitral Tribunal on February 14, 1927, the Tribunal held that while there was no precise rule of prescription in international law, the principle was "an integral and necessary part of every system of law," and stability and security in human affairs required that a time should be fixed after which it would not be permitted to invoke rights or obligations. The Tribunal accordingly barred the claim on the principle of prescription.[36]

It is often urged that adjudication should be developed into a more widely used procedure for handling claims for changes in the status quo. The reasons why this is considered as desirable are two. In the first place, judicial bodies are generally regarded as more detached and disinterested than other international agencies, and hence there is hope that nations will be willing to entrust more important matters to them. In the second place, decisions of judicial tribunals are binding on the parties, whereas the existing procedures of peaceful change are voluntary and depend on persuasion, and are often for that reason ineffective. Proposals looking toward

[35] *Opinions of Commissioners,* Feb. 4, 1926, to July 23, 1927, p. 311.

[36] *Annual Digest of Public International Law Cases,* 1927-8, Case No. 173. See on this point Lauterpacht, *op. cit.* Chaps. IV-VI and F. S. Dunn, *The Protection of Nationals* (Baltimore, 1932), Chap. V.

increasing the use of adjudication in peaceful change usually provide for some means of allowing judicial tribunals to escape from the limitations of the law and to decide claims on some other basis. Most frequently it is proposed that tribunals be given greater power to decide in accordance with "equity" or *"ex aequo et bono."*

These proposals reveal some confusion in regard to the nature of equity. To the extent that equity is conceived of as involving a notion of justice that is different from and outside of the existing system of law, the proposals seem both superfluous and confusing. Courts given the power to decide in accordance with equity are not expected to depart from the existing legal system nor do they do so in practice.[37] By recourse to "general principles of law" or to "higher law" the existing body of international law can be made sufficiently flexible to meet the requirements of equity and justice, in whatever manner these terms may be conceived. It is not even necessary that a court be given the power to decide in accordance with equity, although specific instructions to this effect may sometimes lead to a slightly broader view of the purpose of the law.

Where a court is specially endowed with the authority to decide *"ex aequo et bono"* there seems to be some intention on the part of the parties that it shall go outside the existing body of law for its

[37]Cf. Lauterpacht, *op. cit.,* p. 314.

decision if it deems that necessary in the fulfillment of justice. But it is not to be supposed that the parties intended the court to decide arbitrarily or capriciously. Presumably the court will have reference to some norms of social welfare in reaching its decision. It seems to be free, nevertheless, to change existing legal rights if that is necessary. To this extent the tribunal has clearly been endowed with legislative powers and can operate as an agency of peaceful change.

In the absence of an effective international legislature there is undoubtedly much to be gained in endowing international tribunals on occasion with definite legislative power. But this must be done with great care lest it result merely in discouraging nations from using the judicial process. In the first place there should be some understanding as to the criteria which should guide tribunals in the exercise of the legislative function, in order that less room should be allowed for the operation of bias and prejudice. In the second place, the practice of giving courts the power to decide *ex aequo et bono* should be confined to *ad hoc* agreements and should not be included in general agreements of compulsory arbitration. In the case of *ad hoc* agreements the parties are aware of the circumstances and presumably have some idea of what interests would be affected if the court were given legislative powers. In the case of a general system of compulsory adjudication, the parties would have no check on the court and could not safeguard themselves in matters which they deemed vital. In the view of Professor Lauterpacht, the "mere possibility of such a power being exercised must reduce the authority and usefulness of the existing rules of international law."[38]

[38]Lauterpacht, *op. cit.*, p. 328.

CHAPTER FIVE

CONCLUSIONS

THE procedures discussed in the last chapter are the only legally recognized procedures available at the present time for peaceful changes in the status quo. The notable thing about them is that they are voluntary procedures. The things to be changed, on the other hand, are for the most part things which are highly valued and not willingly given up by existing holders. This fact cannot be disguised by any multiplication of specific institutions and techniques for dealing with demands for change. The widespread notion that by the mere calling of conferences, the establishment of international commissions of inquiry or the devising of new techniques of negotiation it will be possible to find acceptable solutions for all demands for change is largely the product of wishful thinking. It is useless to pile up additional institutions unless they take full account of existing values and attitudes which determine national policies. In this connection one might well recall Fleury's well-known admonition to the Abbé Saint-Pierre after reading the latter's "Project of Perpetual Peace." "You have forgotten an essential article," said Fleury, "that of dispatching missionaries to touch the hearts of princes and to persuade them to enter into your views."

It is idle to spend time devising procedures and institutions of peaceful change which would work if only nations were more rational or less nationalistic than they are. If they were, the procedures would not be necessary. Prudence would seem to require that, in devising institutions which are necessarily voluntary in character, one should take some account of the fundamental aims and desires of national governments. Little as we know about the ways of persuasion, that is the field in which institutions of peaceful change must for the most part operate.

Much time and disappointment can be saved by eliminating from consideration the types of situation in which nations are not going to be persuaded, except by the actual use of force. As suggested in Chapter I, this would include all situations which involved a drastic alteration in the power relationships of nations. The reason why these situations are beyond the reach of mechanisms of persuasion is that self-help is still the ultimate means of making the national will prevail in international matters, and nations will not voluntarily yield up what power they may have either to defend themselves or to exert their will over other nations. It seems impossible, in other words, to devise effective international institutions or techniques to deal with such conflicts so long as paramount force is not at the command of the international community. The same is true of many demands for change which, although based on genuine peace-time needs, would nevertheless involve a definite shift of power.

The question of power likewise enters into the operation of procedures of peaceful change by persuasion. Many changes in the status quo have been effected in the past by procedures which are presumably addressed to the reason or the self-interest of the nation asked to yield to a proposed change, but the result is too often an accurate reflection of the relative power positions of the parties. This would not be so unfortunate, perhaps, if the changes effected were in the general interest of the parties or of the international community and hence offered a more satisfactory basis for enduring peaceful relations. But too often they have been conceived in the immediate interest of the state having the power advantage. The resulting peace is only a temporary truce while the nation which was forced to acquiesce is gaining strength to challenge the settlement. Thus it is quite true that the Congress of Berlin peacefully brought about a set of changes in the status quo and prevented an immediate war, but some of its terms, such as the disposition of Bosnia and Herzegovina, merely laid the groundwork for the greater catastrophe of 1914.

Under present conditions the only demands for changes in the status quo which receive the serious consideration of the international community are those which involve a threat of disturbance of peace if not satisfied. Procedures for effecting changes are customarily thought of in terms of such threats, rather than in terms of the needs of individual states. Thus the demands which have given rise to current discussions of peaceful change are all demands of Great Powers. One does not hear much discussion, for example, of the possibility that a country like Switzerland might be suffering from a lack of raw materials, or that China might need more territory in order to obtain relief from population pressure, or that Austria should have colonies in order to provide her with markets for her surplus manufactures. The specific claims discussed are those of nations which are in a position to threaten war if their demands are not conceded.

This situation seems to be the inevitable reflection of the present stage of development of international society. Most alterations of the status quo require some kind of pressure to bring them about. Great Powers can generally supply the pressure themselves. In the case of small Powers, the pressure has to be supplied by the community or some part of it. At the present time, the consciousness of community interest is weak. The only general interest which seems to be persuasive and convincing to the point of action is the need for peace. This is especially true since the pressure which may be necessary to bring about a particular change may carry with it a threat of war. Eventually it may be possible to build up a general community interest in the welfare of individual members, a realization that community welfare depends on the satisfaction of the needs of individual members. But at the present time the only motivating interest of the community in the needs of individual states is the general desire to avoid war.

The discussion of specific current demands for change in the status quo led to certain general conclusions. In the first place, the proposal to placate the dissatisfied Powers or bribe them into keeping the peace by yielding to their demands, one by one, appears to be fully discredited. There is no reason to suppose that the dissatisfied Powers could by this means be made permanently satisfied with their lot, except by yielding to them enough to assure them a superior power position. Only in this manner would they be certain to achieve a feeling of security and "equality" with the Powers now enjoying an advantageous position. But this would mean merely a reversal of positions among the Great Powers and the struggle for paramountcy would be continued.

Nor can peace be purchased by exchanging or redistributing colonies among the Powers. Proposals of this kind imply that colonies are things to be exploited exclusively for the benefit of the mother country. But this view is in direct conflict with current efforts to reëstablish the system of international trade and would encourage the continuation of preference schemes and other obstacles to that trade. Furthermore, this view implies an attitude of indifference toward the welfare of the native inhabitants of colonial territories. Finally, it raises problems of defence of such territories and of protection of the lines of communication with the mother country.

The conclusion seems clear that the present difficulties of the dissatisfied Powers cannot be permanently overcome by giving them empires. On the contrary, the most promising way to meet these difficulties seems to be to turn away from the idea of empire altogether and toward the idea of a freer international trade with all countries. In other words, instead of perpetuating the notion of exclusive exploitation of colonial territories, the world needs to move in the direction of a liquidation of existing colonial empires.

Consideration was given to the lack of raw materials and to population pressure as grounds for possible changes in the status quo. The general conclusion was reached that, while neither of these grounds offered in itself a convincing case for transfer of territory, certain countries undoubtedly were suffering from adverse conditions in these respects which might possibly be alleviated to some extent by international action.

Thus in the case of raw materials it appears that, in spite of all that is said about the availability of raw materials in the open market, the industrialized countries which lack essential raw material sources have grounds for feelings of insecurity on two counts; (1) they are at the mercy of possible monopolistic and discriminatory practices of the producers, and (2) their ability to continue purchasing depends primarily on the effective working of the international monetary system.

In regard to the first ground, it is doubtless true that the actual damage done to consumers to date by monopolistic schemes and discriminatory practices in general has not been as great as might have been anticipated, considering the number of attempts that have been made. But the number is growing and the techniques are constantly improving, so that the unprotected consuming countries have grounds to feel uneasy. The remedies suggested in Chapter II were (1) the development of a code of fair practice in the exploitation of essential raw materials, and (2) consumer representation on all production control schemes.

The suggestion of the development of a code of fair practices has often been made. Messrs. Wallace and Edminster regard it as the most feasible solution of the problem of raw materials.[1] The

[1] B. B. Wallace and L. R. Edminster, *International Control of Raw Materials* (Washington, 1930), p. 318.

problem involves both the formulation of rules of fair practice that would be generally acceptable and the interpretation and enforcement of these rules in particular cases. The first, so long as acceptance of the rules remains voluntary, will be much easier to accomplish than the second. Nations have been extremely wary of any international schemes which sought to limit or control national economic policy in any way. Nevertheless, as a price of getting rid of the problem of raw materials, nations might be willing to make a small start in this direction.

A suggestion is found in the machinery devised to control the illicit trade in opium. This is one of the few cases in which, by persistent effort, it has been possible to induce nations to accept some degree of supervision by an international agency in a matter of economic interest. The machinery in this case consists primarily of an Advisory Committee, composed of twenty-five members and two assessors, which represents both the producing or manufacturing countries and the consuming countries, and a Permanent Central Opium Board, composed of eight experts who are independent of their governments. The former aids the Council of the League in the general supervision over existing agreements regarding opium and other dangerous drugs. The latter is authorized to keep a constant watch on the movements of the international drug market, and where it appears that a particular country is accumulating excessive supplies the Board may ask for explanations. If the explanations are unsatisfactory it may recommend that the Council of the League apply certain sanctions provided for in the Opium Convention of 1925.

As a means of preventing abuses in the distribution of raw materials and of giving assurance of equal access to the sources of raw materials, a similar machinery might be set up. This might consist of an advisory body of government representatives and a small commission of independent experts. The advisory body would be composed of representatives of both the producing and consuming countries. It would have the task of drawing up provisions of a code of fair practices in the exploitation and distribution of raw materials, such a code to be submitted to the various governments for approval in the usual way. The duty of the board of experts would be to keep close watch on all control schemes and restrictive measures which tended to obstruct access to raw materials, and to report on any apparent violations of the code of fair practices to the advisory body. In the beginning at least it would probably not be possible to give the advisory body power to act in any way save through publicity. However, that on occasion might be a very useful weapon. For example, if it were revealed that a particular control scheme was tending toward monopoly advantage, the consumers might be organized to fight it. But the important part of the scheme would be the development of a common body of opinion as to what was fair practice in the exploitation and distribution of raw materials.

The matter of consumer representation on particular control schemes would doubtless have to be left to the voluntary action of the organizers of such schemes. However, if there were in existence some such machinery as described above to give publicity to control schemes, it would be easy to develop opposition to particular schemes which failed to give representation to consumers and which threatened to take unfair advantage of them.

There remains the problem of how nations without raw materials are going to purchase them when there is a breakdown of the international trade system and an inability to obtain the necessary foreign exchange. This is the situation roughly in which Germany finds herself today. While it is true that her continued foreign exchange stringency is due in part to obstacles which she herself has placed against the free movement of commerce, she is by no means the only offender, nor could she by her own actions restore her trade to its former level. Pending the resumption of more normal conditions in her foreign trade, Germany will continue to suffer from an inability to obtain the foreign exchange with which to buy raw materials.

As suggested in Chapter II, this problem may be approached as one of foreign credits. Let us assume that Germany's economic welfare depends in large measure on her ability to sell manufactured goods abroad. She manufactures these goods out of raw materials which also come from abroad. In other words, she needs to purchase raw materials abroad in order to sell manufactured goods abroad. Since both transactions take place abroad, there would seem to be no particular reason for using Germany's limited supply of foreign exchange in the process. All that is needed is to provide sufficient foreign credit to cover the purchase of the raw material until liquidated through the sale of the manufactured goods. This would give Germany the necessary purchasing power to acquire raw materials, quite apart from her ability to raise foreign exchange. The proceeds from the sale of manufactured goods abroad, after paying for the raw materials, could be used for the purchase of foodstuffs and other products to be consumed at home, or for the liquidation of Germany's external indebtedness. In this manner Germany might be brought back into the system of international trade quite as successfully, perhaps, as if she were given territory containing sources of the raw materials she needs.

This plan seems to offer a promising method of attack upon the problem of Germany's inability to purchase raw materials, but there are two points about it which present some difficulty. The first is the source of the proposed credits and the second is the recapturing of her foreign markets for her manufactured goods.

In the beginning, at least, the necessary credits would doubtless have to be granted by governments or at least insured by them. The uncertainties of the situation are such that private credit would very likely not be available except at exorbitant rates. But if governments supplied the credits, Germany might be fearful that they might be used for ulterior purposes, for example, to gain political concessions from her. There would have to be ample assurances that the plan would be looked upon as a straightforward commercial transaction and no political advantages would be sought from it. This would doubtless require supervision by some international agency in which Germany was represented equally with the lending states. Such a function might very well be entrusted to the Bank for International Settlements. For this purpose, only slight changes would seem to be necessary in its constitution and organization.

In any event, the whole scheme postulates a greater expectation of markets for German manufactures than exists at the present moment. Even granted credit with which to buy raw materials, German manufacturers would still have to compete with those of other countries for markets. Countries already in possession of markets would not relinquish them without a struggle. In many cases existing markets are protected by tariffs, bilateral agreements, etc. As things stand, Germany's greatest hope would be the creation of new markets, presumably in present backward countries. It is true that her increased purchase of raw materials would itself create a certain amount of new international purchasing power, some of which would undoubtedly be turned Germany's way. However, any important enlargement of Germany's markets would seem to be contingent on the breaking down of trade barriers and a general revival of international trade.

But even if Germany were assured access to raw material sources by these methods, she would still desire the return of her colonies. The reasons are (1) markets and (2) honor.

In regard to the question of markets, it is often urged that colonies are an economic burden rather than an asset, and that to return Germany's colonies to her would not help her economic situation. Thus Grover Clark produces figures to show that during the twenty years in which Germany had her colonies, 1894-1913, her total trade with them (including Kiaochao) was 972 million marks, whereas her colonial expenses during the same period (not including those for Kiaochao) were 1,002 million marks.[2] His conclusion is that Germany's colonies cost her far more than any possible profits she could have derived from them.

But Dr. Schacht regards as "particularly ridiculous" the assertion that Germany's former colonies are valueless and it would do Germany no good if they were returned to her. "This immediately prompts the retort: If the colonies are so bad, why do you keep them?"[3] He points out that before the war free trade prevailed on a large scale and that Germany had valuable foreign investments, so that it was not necessary for her to develop her colonies with particular energy. Even so she did far better with her colonies than other countries which had had colonies much longer. Today, when free trade no longer exists in the world, when Germany is struggling with heavy foreign debts and lacks the foreign exchange with which to buy raw materials, she would naturally proceed to develop her colonies with far greater intensity.

Dr. Schacht might also have pointed to the figures which show that colonial imports, even in "open door" areas, are headed by those from the mother country, and that the same is true even in a number of the mandates. In any case he is undoubtedly correct in saying that the record of German colonial development before the war is a very

[2]Grover Clark, *The Balance Sheets of Imperialism* (New York, 1936), p. 11.

[3]*Foreign Affairs, op. cit.,* p. 230.

poor indication of what Germany would do if she had her colonies now.

Equally important is the subject of German honor. Germany feels undeniably humiliated over the fact that her colonies were taken away from her and that she alone of the Great Powers is not regarded as worthy to have a colonial empire. This feeling is expressed as merely a desire for equality with the other Great Powers, or as a desire to remove the only remaining sign of defeat and dishonor as incorporated in the peace treaties. This could be accomplished, it is said, either by giving Germany back her colonies or by the other powers giving up theirs.

It is probably true that Germany's demand for her colonies will continue to be a source of unrest until some move is made by the other Powers to make her feel that she has been restored to a place of equality in this matter. But outright restoration would not seem to be an appropriate solution, because that would upset the distribution of power in Africa and would imply at the same time a cavalier treatment of native populations. It would likewise provide a distinct threat to Great Britain's control of the sea route around Africa, because it would provide Germany with possible naval and air bases in Africa from which that route might be attacked. Much the same objection might be raised against the proposal to make Germany the mandatory power over her former colonies. For the international controls at present embodied in the mandates system are not sufficient to prevent mandated territories from being used for war purposes.

It has been suggested that a possible way of restoring Germany's honor and self-respect in this matter without adding to her relative power position would be to conduct an experiment in international administration of colonial territory. According to the suggestion, certain territory in Africa would be set aside for development by common action of the Powers. The specific territory would have to be decided upon later by some impartial body, but in any case it would come from several different holders. This territory would be administered as an international protectorate, under the authority of an international body on which Germany would be represented on an equal plane with the other Powers.

The main points which would require close attention in any such scheme would be the following: (1) the internationalization of the local administration should be undertaken very gradually in order to lessen the inconvenience and confusion of the change for the existing population; (2) the members of the international commission set up to guide the experiment should have ample authority to inspect the territory and receive complaints; (3) contracts and concessions should be entered into only with the approval of the international commission; (4) raw materials existing in quantity in the territory should be exploited under the supervision of the international commission; and (5) the territory should be placed under the protection of an international guarantee[4].

It is possible that a scheme of this kind, if it worked reasonably well, would be extended to other territories. In any case it should go far toward satisfying Germany's claim to equality without at the same time increasing her war strength at the expense of the holders of her former colonies. It would likewise offer a test of the sincerity of the opposition to Germany's colonial claims which rests on the ground that the present holders are "trustees" for the native inhabitants and hence are not in a position to relinquish their control. An international régime of the kind suggested would provide a more certain assurance against exploitation of the native population than would control by any one state.

In general, what would most help Germany solve her problems of raw materials and markets would be a genuine revival of the system of international trade, with Germany participating actively in the system. This would have to come about primarily

[4]It is interesting in connection with this scheme to recall that the American Secretary of State at the time of the Berlin Conference of 1884-5 suggested that the Congo Basin be neutralized and "held in trust for the benefit of all peoples." (Samuel Flagg Bemis, *A Diplomatic History of the United States,* New York, 1936, p. 570.)

through national action of individual states in removing barriers to trade and intercourse in general. This subject has been fully treated in Professor Staley's study and will not be dealt with here, except to endorse the findings of that study. But under the best possible conditions, progress in this direction is bound to be slow. As Staley has pointed out:

> On account of the vested interests and established expectations which have grown up around the system of import barriers in every country, lessening of these barriers will come about slowly, if at all, and reductions should be carefully planned so as to minimize the shocks of readjustment that must be inflicted upon established high-cost enterprises.[5]

In the field of bilateral action, the strongest possible endorsement should be given to Secretary Hull's reciprocal trade agreement program. Even more important than the gains resulting from specific reductions in tariff walls, is the psychological effect of this program in inducing a number of nations to think in terms of lowering tariff barriers rather than raising them. Furthermore, the generalizing of the benefits of these agreements through the use of the unconditional most-favored-nation clause is in noteworthy contrast to the practice of Germany and other states of treating foreign trade as a matter of bilateral bargaining.

In the field of multilateral action an extremely helpful step toward general recovery was the cur-

[5]Staley, *op. cit.*, p. 185.

rency agreement reached in September, 1936, between the United States, Great Britain, and France, and concurred in by a number of other states.

It is often proposed that more effective international machinery should be built up to deal with the economic relations of nations and to aid in the restoration of the system of international trade. Frequently it is urged that the Economic Committee of the League of Nations could be made into a more effective agency if it were given greater autonomy. The most popular suggestion is to erect a separate organization for this purpose that would stand in the same relation to the League of Nations as does the International Labor Organization.

At the time of the Paris Peace Conference, a number of proposals were made for establishing intergovernmental economic and financial organizations. A proposal was made to set up a financial section of the League, but this did not get beyond the early drafts of the Covenant. President Wilson's second draft carried a "Declaration for Equality of Trade Conditions," providing against discriminating tariffs and dumping. A note attached by the Technical Advisers stated that "Provisions for an International Trade Commission, regarded as a desirable, if not an essential, part of a declaration of this character, are under preparation."[6]

[6]Miller, *op. cit.*, II, 18, and I, 22.

However, these provisions were not forthcoming and Wilson's third and fourth drafts merely forbade discrimination.[7] Various proposals were made by other delegations, but the provision on this subject that finally was included in the Covenant was very vague. Article 23, paragraph (e) provided as follows:

> Subject to and in accordance with the provisions of international conventions existing or hereafter to be agreed upon, the Members of the League: . . .
>
> (e) will make provision to secure and maintain freedom of communications and of transit and equitable treatment for the commerce of all Members of the League. . . .

At the Economic Conference held in 1927 Mr. Arthur Pugh made a proposal which had been adopted by the British Labour Party at its annual conference in 1927. This proposal was to the effect that the Economic Section of the League of Nations should be developed along lines roughly analogous to those of the I.L.O. "An Economic Council, representative of states, producers (including employers and workers), and consumers should be established. It should consider the Surveys and Reports made from time to time by the Economic Secretariat. It should formulate policy in International Economic Conventions or by means of Recommendations. It

[7]Miller, *op. cit.*, II, 105, 154.

should, of course, work in close coöperation with the I.L.O. and other activities of the League."[8]

At the same time M. Jouhaux, the French trade union representative and member of the Governing Body of the International Labor Organization, proposed a semi-autonomous economic organization, consisting of a Conference—representing finance, agriculture, commerce, labor, coöperatives and consumers—and an Executive Council of eighteen members, twelve being appointed by the Council of the League and six by the Governing Body of the International Labor Organization, three members from its employers' and three from its labor groups.[9]

A Committee appointed to study the "Constitution, Procedure and Practice of Committees of the League of Nations," reporting in 1935, seemed to

[8]Quoted in H. R. G. Greaves, *Raw Materials and International Control* (London, 1936), p. 5.

[9]*Ibid.*, pp. 25-6. Greaves himself has made a proposal of an Economic Council of Ministers of Commerce: "A council which brought the ministers of commerce regularly together would have a high level of debate, and probably a considerable output of work. It might also be expected to develop a sense of unity which would give it a vital importance in international affairs. Were it supplied with responsible work to do, were it to operate in the publicity which would naturally be given to such a meeting of responsible ministers, there can be small doubt that it would tend to develop an *esprit de corps* of its own, which might have great significance in the work of the League. And even if this were not so it would bring before ministers at first hand the personal views of those actually responsible for framing policy in other countries. It would often give them this contact at a time before the definite lines of their policy had been laid down. Experience has shown that agreement comes more easily at this early stage. Opinions are then more flexible and less involved in questions of prestige or 'losing face'." (*The League Committees and World Order,* Oxford, 1931, p. 61.)

be impressed with the need for giving greater authority and coördination to the work of the technical organizations, in particular to the Economic and Financial Committees. In this connection the Committee said, "there is no reason why the League should not seek, when the matter is of sufficient importance, to solve economic and financial problems through the effective collaboration of Ministers of Finance and Economics, in the same way as Foreign Ministers collaborate in the Council to solve political problems."

Again,

> It is essential that both the effective initiative and the control in regard to the undertakings and carrying out of different tasks should be in the hands of the Governments. The Council and the Assembly will constitutionally be in the supreme control but it is expedient that, within the general framework of action approved by them, specialized bodies of Government representatives should control different spheres of work.
>
> It is within the lines so determined that "expert" or "technical" bodies must work.
>
> A technical Committee must not be prevented from bringing a given question to the notice of the Council or Assembly and proceeding, for that purpose, to discuss it in preliminary fashion. Such preliminary discussion, however, should not proceed to the point of committing the League to new responsibilities (establishing new organs, enquiries, etc.) until the authority of the Council or Assembly has been given.

The Committee seemed to feel that the League's economic sphere of action should be broadened. As regards the existing Economic Committee, it approved in general the constitution of the Economic Committee as revised in 1927 "subject to the consideration that a general programme is framed by a governmental body, and that special provision is made for tasks which do not fall within the Economic Committee's normal sphere," *i.e.,* international commercial relations. "In such cases, special committees might be set up, reporting direct to the Council."

In concluding its report, the Committee said:

In the first place, the Committee agrees that there should be a clear distinction between the adoption of general plans, co-ordination, direction and control on the one hand and executive work on the other, the former being recognized as a governmental matter and the latter as a technical one. Secondly, the Committee has recommended that the system of appointing, as far as possible, special committees for specific tasks should be developed in practice.

If these principles are endorsed by the Council and the Assembly and put into application, it seems to follow as a natural consequence (especially in view of the information the Committee has obtained regarding the procedure and practice of the various League organizations) that appropriate steps must be taken to set in motion, direct and co-ordinate the work of the various special Committees.

This would suggest that suitable arrangements should be made, in some form to be decided upon, for drawing up a programme of work and co-ordinating and supervising its execution on such lines as to secure the necessary governmental authority.[10]

The 1935 Assembly considered the report but did not see fit to adopt the suggestion for setting up new intergovernmental machinery.[11]

We have considered above certain specific demands for changes in the status quo which threaten the peace of the world and possible ways of dealing with these demands peacefully. Let us now return briefly to the general subject of procedures of peaceful change and consider whether it is not possible, within the framework outlined in Chapter IV, to devise some more effective means of weighing proposals for changes in the status quo.

One difficulty with the present situation is that none of the existing procedures was designed especially for dealing with questions of change. They have been developed primarily to deal with *disputes* between nations, particularly disputes over rights and interests. Hence in making use of these existing procedures to discuss proposals of peaceful change, the tendency is strong to look upon them as disputes, which means that attitudes of defense are immediately aroused. Questions of power and national policies arise to obstruct the consideration

[10] *Report of the Committee Appointed to Study the Constitution, Procedure, and Practice of Committees of the League of Nations.* (A. 16. 1935.)

[11] Cf. *Official Journal,* Special Supplement 140, p. 84. Another suggestion is that of a world consular service, advanced by Professor Staley in his book entitled *War and the Private Investor* (New York, 1935), pp. 510-514.

of the proposal on its merits or from the standpoint of the general welfare of the community. Public opinion in each country becomes focused on the necessity of protecting the national interest before it becomes possible to explore the situation in terms of the general welfare.

In order to overcome this difficulty it is suggested that a special procedure be adopted for consideration of proposals of changes in the status quo. This procedure should be as unofficial and informal as possible in order to allow some investigation and consideration before national attitudes had become crystallized. To this end it is suggested that small unofficial standing committees be set up in each country for the preliminary consideration of proposals of change in the status quo. These committees would act in a purely advisory capacity, their function being to explore the proposals from all possible angles, including both power relationships and the general welfare, and to make recommendations privately to their respective governments. They would have the right to communicate directly with the committees in the other countries concerned with the proposal and to seek agreement, if possible, on some common recommendation. But it would be necessary that these preliminary explorations be conducted without publicity in order that national attitudes might not become fixed before an opportunity had been given to discuss possible solutions.

It has been pointed out that bilateral agreements providing for changes in the status quo are often suspected of being directed against third states.[12] This difficulty might be obviated in the proposed scheme by allowing the committees of the states directly concerned in a particular proposal to consult privately with the committees in all the other states whose interests were likely to be affected in any way. Such consultation would likewise serve to reveal any general interest of the international community that might be involved in the proposed change.

The successful operation of a procedure of this sort would depend in large degree upon the personnel of the several committees. They should be people of some eminence in their communities in order that their recommendations should carry weight. Preferably they should not be diplomatists by profession since the habitual activity of the diplomatist is to defend the interests of his own state and this makes it somewhat difficult for him to consider proposed changes in the status quo except in terms of national interest. They should not hold public office since that would imply that in their investigations they were acting under instructions from their respective governments, whereas the chief value of their recommendations would rest in the independ-

[12]Cf. David Mitrany, "Territorial Revision and Article 19 of the League Covenant," *International Affairs*, November-December, 1935, Vol. 14, p. 834.

ence and detachment of the investigators. It would be inadvisable to use for this purpose any existing mechanism for dealing with disputes between nations, such as the national groups of the Permanent Court of Arbitration at the Hague, since the object is to have proposals for change dealt with in a manner different from that in which disputes over rights are treated.

A plan of this sort would not guarantee that all proposals for change would be settled peacefully and in the general interest. It would not alter the fact that procedures of change are procedures of persuasion, and that questions of power usually prevail over other considerations. But it would provide an opportunity for investigation and the consideration of possible solutions in a calmer atmosphere than that which has usually prevailed in such cases in the past, and would make it possible to point out the general interest before individual national interests had become too firmly set. This would greatly facilitate the marshalling of support for solutions favorable to the general welfare and also the unifying of opposition to projects that threaten the peace of the community. That would be a great advance over the machinery that now exists for the consideration of claims for changes in the status quo.

INDEX